THE GOLDEN RULES OF SOCIAL MEDIA MARKETING

#THEGOLDENRULES

HEATHER HEUMAN

Hardcover
978-1-64184-182-5

Paperback
978-1-64184-183-2

ebook
978-1-64184-184-9

To my husband, Wayne Heuman.
Thank you for being the man of God you are and for loving this quirky girl from South Carolina.

To my children,
Mahaley, Jules, and Fulton.
I love you to the moon and back. Thanks for giving me the title of mom, the greatest joy!

Contents

Foreword

There is no shortcut for social media marketing success.

I wish I could be the one to tell you that all you need is a Facebook page and two hundred fans to succeed in business but—no.

In fact, I've been in marketing for more than thirty years and can say with authority that there has never been a more challenging time to be in business. Our customers are fragmented, their attention is interminably distracted, and our means of reaching them has splintered into a thousand media shards.

A new generation of digital natives are unreachable—even proudly unreachable—by our traditional marketing methods.

Sure, social media marketing can work, but it has also become a victim of its own success. The more that companies pile on, the harder it is to cut through the clutter and become a signal instead of more noise.

There is no marketing easy button in this era of infinite

media. It is grind, grind, grind, and iterate. Grind, grind, grind, and iterate.

That's the beauty of this book. Heather doesn't pull any punches or make any false promises. There are no rainbow-flavored expectations here. This is solid social media marketing advice forged from the trenches.

Heather knows what works and generously shares her wisdom with her characteristic southern charm. Get out your notebook, buy a new highlighter, pour a glass of sweet tea, and get ready for some social media truths.

Mark Schaefer
Author of *Marketing Rebellion: The Most Human Company Wins*

Introduction

I received a call from my friend asking if I was accepting new clients. A quick glance at my calendar, "well, actually yes, I do have some space for new clients!" She replied, "Great! I'm going to introduce you to someone."

The thought set aside, I went about my day doing the things a mom does that operates a business out of a home office: working with my regular clients, working on my Social Thrive Business Academy, and preparing a pot roast with roasted asparagus for dinner.

The friend request on Facebook came later in the day from the gentleman who wanted to talk. We jumped on Messenger for a quick conversation and verified a good time to connect. Our phone conversation of fifteen minutes confirmed my organic Facebook growth services were a good fit for him as well as my prices.

"Great," he said. "When can we start?"

It was literally that simple. And with the power of social media, I made $72,000 in eleven months from that one client.

You see, my friend who referred me to this new client is someone I had only known one year through Facebook. This might seem like a simple thing, but getting new clients equals increased revenue for my company. It gives my husband and I the ability to say we're creating the life we really want as opposed to the one we can afford, including private school options for our kids and growing our team so we can serve our clients and students better.

But this friend of mine that made the referral knew my quality of work, knew the results I get my clients, and she knew that I'd be a good fit personally. This warm introduction was possible because of relationships created and cultivated on Facebook.

Over the years, my business has grown far enough that I can be picky about the clients I want to work with instead of saying yes to whoever comes knocking. It allows me direct control of my time, connections with many wonderful people, all of which has a huge impact on the direction of my business and attracts opportunities for more, both personally and professionally.

I'm sharing this because I want you to know you can have it, too. It doesn't matter where you come from, how much money you do or don't have, or if your business is 30 minutes or 30 years old.

Wherever you're starting from, the power of social media marketing can revolutionize your entire business. Leads can and will come your way by the relationships and connections you make and foster. You can create more visibility and have more people thinking of you when you can provide them solutions for the problems they face.

We could talk for hours and hours about social media, and in fact, that's the purpose behind this entire book. I want to share with you what I've learned along the way, how you can use it to your advantage, and have it all collected so you can come back and reference it as often as you like.

It's time to remove limiting mindsets. You don't need a marketing department the size of Target and Starbucks. Your desire to have a thriving business or to create opportunities for your family through your business is absolutely possible, and social media can help you get there that much faster when done the right way.

Four quick notes:

1) Please understand that social media is *not* some magic pill for your business. Though it can drastically improve your results, it still requires our proper attention and done properly is more a marathon, not a sprint. Enduring businesses are based on long-term relationships and healthy connections. Consider this your move in the direction of your legacy and behave accordingly.

2) We're covering all the basics you need here in the book. To stay current on all things social media marketing for business building, I encourage you to check out my *Business, Jesus and Sweet Tea* podcast.

3) I'm a strategy girl! What I share in this book helped me build my own businesses from zero to profitable with a six-figure income and has helped me do the same for others. I am excited you're here, and I'm going to tell you everything about using social media marketing the right way.

4) Since we are trying to help you be more social, anything you read that jumps off the pages as super helpful, let me know on social media by using our hashtag for the book #thegoldenrules and using @heatherheuman, too. I look forward to being social right back with you. 🔥

And with that out of the way, I encourage you to grab a cold glass of sweet tea (it is, after all the finest beverage on the entire planet. Scientific fact…) or any other suitable drink you'd prefer and get ready to take lots of notes on what we're about to share.

A Quick Backstory

It might sound like an overstatement to suggest to you that social media dramatically changed my life, but that's the actual truth.

Injuries he sustained in Iraq, coupled with years of foot injuries, forced my husband, Wayne, out of the military in 2010 and they offered to relocate us one last time to help us transition into our new life. Well, almost. Wayne found a position as a civilian contractor working for the Human Resource Command for the U.S. Army in Elizabethtown, Kentucky. Accordingly, we found ourselves on the outskirts of Fort Knox, Kentucky, with a five-year-old getting ready to go into kindergarten, a one-year-old, and a six-week-old baby. I had a desire to homeschool, but two young ones at home and one in kindergarten would have been enough to put me over the edge.

We decided not to homeschool that year but soon realized we needed some extra income in our family. My husband suggested I go back to graduate school, which I did in spite of some concerns about the kids and the time commitment. My husband's military GI benefits would foot the bill, and after fourteen months, I ended up earning a Master of Arts in Management and Leadership. I didn't realize it at the time, but that was probably the biggest transforming part of my adult life that I ever have experienced. It turns out that I absolutely *loved* business, and I'm so thankful to God for using my wonderful husband to push me in ways I might otherwise never have pursued.

So much so that I decided to create my own company because I couldn't be the wife and mom I wanted to be if I were to leave the kids in daycare while I worked for someone else. That wasn't an option for me because it had always been my childhood and lifelong dream to stay home with my children while they were young.

"But what to do," I quizzed myself. What do I have a passion for and what was I good at that could form a sustainable business?

I thought about it for a while and kept coming back to my experience of the moves we made while in the military. In each of those moves, I would create Yahoo Groups online for the other military moms with young children. These wonderful little communities brought us together where we could easily find connections, make friends, and cultivate play-date opportunities with great women like Jessica, Ashley, Karen, and Alyssa.

Eventually, I expanded the content in the group to help the moms know how they could get to local happenings, parks, and other things to do with their children. For example, during our stay in Germany, I found this wonderful Mexican restaurant and shared directions, including photos so everyone could go enjoy the amazing food while living in Wiesbaden, Germany. It brought me such joy sharing shortcuts, tips, and anything else I could to bring people together and make their lives easier.

As I sat there in my graduate classes, contemplating these things and wondering about the business I could create, it occurred to me I had a model I could monetize. Thus, I pretty much stumbled upon my first business: a go-to resource for busy families with children ages 20 to 50 that lived within a 30-mile radius of Elizabethtown. To keep it simple and easy to understand, I called it Elizabethtown Family.

It was based on the same idea of those Yahoo groups I created in 2004 in Germany and 2007 in Tennessee: I wanted to create an easy to use, family-friendly resource for working parents and busy people to know about all the fun stuff they could do with their kids.

This seemed like common sense to me, yet the local tourism office didn't offer any resources like this, nor did the local newspaper.

It was a huge gaping hole in the marketplace, and I knew there was a need.

Why all the backstory?

In short, it's to demonstrate that business can be created out of nothing, and we're going to see how social media was so important to expand the brand and amplify the message.

I started this business while I was in the middle of graduate school because the business model was simple. Businesses would pay me to advertise because I was bringing the audience they wanted for customers. Combining this knowledge with my background in digital marketing and web design, I began working on a website for this new venture.

Here's the thing, though...

I created a Facebook business page for Elizabethtown Family, and I just began putting information out to help people until the website would be ready. About all it included was:

- Great places for kids to eat for free
- A local festival that I just found out about
- A place to go rent kayaks at the local park (with the address)

In a nutshell, I used social media first to start generating interest for both the audience and the businesses, first through the Facebook page and then Twitter. The website followed about four months later. It indeed was a credible resource for people brand new to town to learn about the community and all its wonderful offerings. I was also able to demonstrate to businesses genuine public interest, a worthwhile asset in which to invest their marketing dollars, and myself as a helpful and professional resource to help them advertise and grow.

To get the sales, I built a framework with three levels of advertising and a membership directory. That was it. I then reached out to local businesses face to face, asking if they were looking for more exposure to families in the community. It took some grit (as does any business worth pursuing), but I met some fantastic marketing directors, helped them get noticed while gaining recognition for myself, and built wonderful relationships that I still enjoy to this day. The Facebook page is hovering right around 13,000 fans (as of this writing) and continues to serve the community as it was originally intended.

Let's be clear on three critical points:

1) This was not an overnight success. However, it was profitable in less than sixty days, literally from an idea I just had in my head and used the power of social media to build.

2) Elizabethtown is a small community of about 30,000 people. Yet, social media still works to deliver messaging and can create a lasting relationship with your audience, no matter how large or small it may be. Done well over time, your audience will remember you, particularly as you add additional value to their lives, and they will gladly thank you with their patronage.

3) At the end of the day, all business is about people, and we are wise to remember that. Should we forget that and place profits ahead of them, our businesses will eventually begin to falter as our customers go elsewhere to find better service.

But that was just the beginning.

That business, Elizabethtown Family, that I started in 2011, was going well and was very part-time as I was loving the journey of creating a way to build revenue in my company while also being able to take my kids to the park and stay home with my children.

Over time, the business continued to grow, and I expanded by bringing on some amazing women like Jessica Spears. The power of social media once again led to more business growth in my life. After submitting my application to the local chamber along with over sixty applicants, I got the new (and part-time position) as Relationship Manager to help grow the Chamber membership.

Again, the power of social media allowed us to tell more stories about the success of our members and increase our social media strategies to foster business growth goals. Significant growth was well underway in less than ten months. With the permission of the president of the chamber of commerce, I was able to fully run my own company while helping them grow theirs. And little by little, I had business owners reaching out to me asking for help with their social media.

With some very unfortunate circumstances in our personal life in 2013, my husband and I had a shaking realization that life was short, and we were living our lives far from family. No longer did we have the military telling us where our next home would be, yet we were living in Kentucky far from Wayne's family in Missouri/Illinois and farther from my family in South Carolina.

After much prayer, we decided it would be best for our family to pack up and move to South Carolina so we could live closer to my family. Personally, I was thrilled, but professionally, I was a little heartbroken. Everything I had created with social media was in this little bubble in Kentucky. I still ran my Kentucky-based company while I was living in South Carolina but eventually sold it in 2017 after having built it to six figures of revenue. Not too shabby for a part-time business. After a few months of getting settled in our new home in Blythewood, South Carolina, I launched Sweet Tea Social Marketing in 2014. It realized that everything that had happened in my life up until this point was preparing me for this next milestone.

No longer did I have to only serve a thirty-mile radius. Now, I could use the full power of social media marketing and serve business owners across the globe.

I started from scratch, again. I rolled up my sleeves, created new social media profiles on the platforms that I knew could help me build my brand, and I began showing up consistently and serving like crazy. I used social media for five months and had my LinkedIn profile as my home base before my website was complete.

And I just got started. If you learn anything from this book, I want you to realize that "done" is better than "perfect." Make sure you don't quit before you give yourself an opportunity to be found by the exact people who need your product or services.

I began working with clients who trusted my character from face-to-face connections at first. I then began finding clients through Instagram, LinkedIn, Facebook, and even Twitter before six months had even passed. I got way out of my comfort zone and began attending conferences and meeting amazing people like one of my mentors, Kim Garst, and others like Stephanie Nissen, Heather Myklegard, and Dorien Morin-van Dam. I woke up each day knowing that as a social media strategist and speaker I could help driven businesses discover how to grow in today's noisy social marketplace with solid social media strategy because I, too, had done it for myself and others.

I've had the honor of having clients like Chick-fil-A, Wilson Sports, various chambers of commerce, and global brands during my nineteen years in the digital marketing space.

I've been able to leverage social media marketing to build a brand on my terms while creating a lifestyle that honors and allows me to love my husband, Wayne, and kids Mahaley, Jules, and Fulton. What first was enough income to pay for a Disney cruise became consistent revenue that afforded my husband the chance to quit a job he hated and begin his own business in 2016 that is now flourishing.

We stated previously that social media is a marathon, not a sprint. It isn't required to have massive marketing budgets to burn, and there are many reasons why an organic approach can succeed even above paid marketing. We demonstrated earlier that your success might not come overnight, but done right, it can happen quickly and with enduring results.

So, what's your backstory? What experiences have you had that brought you to exactly where you are in your current business, ministry, or non-profit? One thing I know to be true is that what can sometimes feel like the crazy chaos of our lives can often be exactly the experiences we need to thrive in our next season.

This book is designed to help you be seen and be heard by the exact right people you want to serve and who will, in turn, keep you at the forefront of their minds. As you dive into the following chapters, please understand that these methods can work for any kind of business, whether it's local, online, a church, non-profit, or anything else you can imagine. As long as we show up, do our business well, and prioritize people over profits, we can use social media for greater representation and expand our reach much further than we can possibly imagine.

WHO THIS BOOK IS FOR

Are you really about to sit down and check out this book about social media marketing?

Seriously?

Yay!

I'm genuinely excited you're here because I strongly believe that social media marketing can revolutionize the trajectory of your entire organization, brand, ministry, or business. Social media in business and for business by building relationships and fostering community is my passion and brings me tremendous joy in my work.

No doubt I love what I do, but on a personal note, I want you to understand I'm genuinely coming to you as a Christian business owner. Recognizing that might put some people off, it's important for me that you know I believe in putting faith and family as my first priority. And having built two six-figure businesses on the back of social media, I know the opportunity here for you to leverage social media the right way, too.

That's enough about me.

In turn, I want you to know this book is for you if:

- You are a business owner or an entrepreneur yearning to grow your business, and you want to include social media as a part of your marketing strategy
- You feel that nobody sees you or they don't know about your business
- You want to grow your audience and build lasting relationships with people
- You want to use social media to get more visibility and awareness for a stronger customer base
- You find yourself responsible for social media, even if you're not the owner
- You feel like you've been sitting on the sidelines watching others, possibly even your competition, use social media and realize it's time to throw your hat in the ring
- You believe social media is where you need to put more effort into your business
- You already have a successful business with consistent monthly revenue, but you know that there are more people that need your services
- You are ready to show up authentically and don't want to just continue your existing random approach
- You have a local brick and mortar business and know you need to have a stronger social media presence to keep up or even surpass your competition that's already enjoying their social media success

- You provide socially conscious services like education or adoption and want to build more awareness
- You provide professional services like a dental practice or sell Medicare to senior citizens (yes, older people go online, too, and are looking for you)

The list could go on but can be paraphrased that if you want or need to use social media and haven't known where to start, you have the answer in your hands. When we proceed step-by-step, we can remove the fluff (and with it any hints of overwhelm) and create a practical strategy to get you moving in the right direction the first time out.

And as long as we're removing fluff, here's a quick reminder that this isn't some magic pill that removes any need for work so you can retire to Fiji in thirty days. Yes, we can get you the information you need quickly because I like to keep things simple, but please be aware of anyone promising instant results and take their words with the appropriate grain of salt. Sorry to be the killjoy, but I would be remiss if we didn't talk about this.

It's still entirely possible you'll create the perfect viral video that lands you on the *Today Show* or *Ellen*, and if you do, please ask her to stop ignoring my calls as if she doesn't know me (ha ha). That would be amazing if it happens, but it's not a strategy we should rely on.

Instead, let's use this book to remove the mystery of social media and lay the foundational framework to uncover the types of content that can increase the likelihood of going viral. I like to call them the Golden Rules of Social Media Marketing, and I'm excited to share them with you.

The premise of this entire book is based upon my signature S.O.C.I.A.L. framework that can help your business soar with social media marketing the right way.

Let's do this.

What is the S.O.C.I.A.L Framework?

This methodology I created around the acronym S.O.C.I.A.L. was developed to simplify the six critical stages that all business owners need in order to optimize their results using social media for business growth. Let's look really quickly at what this stands for:

S Strong Foundations
O Optimize Relationships
C Choose the Right Platforms
I Influential Content
A Automation and Smart Systems
L Legacy and Kingdom Impact

STAGE ONE

STRONG FOUNDATIONS

Any structure that wants to stand the test of time must be built upon a strong foundation. Our businesses are no different, particularly when it comes to social media for several reasons: we are literally putting ourselves out in front of the world, and accordingly, our behavior will be watched. Even more important, having a well-defined message makes decision making much easier for our audience as well as ourselves.

Rest assured there is much we will cover throughout these pages, but let's make sure we have the following defined before going deeper:

1. **Who are you** – Are you a product or service-based business? What do you stand for?
2. **What you offer** - Identify your business model and offer(s) you will have for people to purchase. What differentiates you in the midst of your competition?

3. **Who you want** - Be clear on who it is you wish to serve. The more specific you are, the better.
4. **What they need** - What are the struggles, pain points, or areas of concern that your customers have that you provide a solution for.

From personal experience, I've seen far too many people struggle because they haven't established this groundwork. Then, deal with undue stress on how to proceed in all areas of business, including what to post on social media. This is so important to business that it's the first element I cover in my Social Thrive Business Academy. After we've built the foundation, it becomes so much easier to leverage the power of social media for growth.

And thus, we come to our first golden rule:

GOLDEN RULE:
Customers Crave For You To Be Clear On How You Can Help Them

IT IS ABOUT THE CUSTOMER, NOT YOU

Perhaps that sounds counterintuitive, particularly since we're the ones building the business. In fact, there are quite a few things about business that sound counterintuitive. Regardless, please follow along through the book before you make any hard-set decisions on how to use this information and what you need to consider in your social media post strategy. Social media offers a new interpretation of how we market, and not everything is as it always was.

Let's expand a bit upon what we started in the last section.

At the risk of contradicting the first paragraph here, it is vital that you understand your business and your offer, including as many strengths as you can possibly come up with. This might sting a bit, but you will do yourself massive favors to find all your weaknesses as well. Your competition will certainly be looking for them and far better to address them ahead of time rather than later.

This exercise will do much to help us better define our messaging and dial in exactly who it is we will be looking to serve. We might think we can serve everybody, but as an example, would a plumber or an electrician be a better person to contact to repair a leaking sink? (Hint: it's not the electrician—ha ha!)

After we've decided who we're going to serve, we need to spend time to understand their wants and desires better. Perhaps you've heard of a customer avatar before, and such strategies are a good start but are limited to only a quick snapshot of who we're trying to reach. They might work to get us started and might be enough depending on what we're offering, but we are wise to dig a little deeper to into the psychology of our audience.

Let's borrow a few of Dan Kennedy's questions from his book *The Ultimate Sales Letter* to help us:

- What keeps them awake at night?
- What are they afraid of?
- What are they angry about? Who are they angry at?
- What are their top three daily frustrations?
- What trends are occurring and will occur in their businesses or lives?
- What do they secretly, ardently desire most?
- Who else is selling something similar to them, and how?

We can add in other questions such as:

- Where do they like to shop?
- What is their family environment like?
- What kind of activities do they enjoy when not using our products and services?

This list could go on for a long time, and it's worth the time to go even further than this. It's crucial we remember that on the other side of that screen is a real person leading a real life and are so much more than just an avatar on a page. They experience joy and frustration, go through life transitions just as we do. The more we can understand and relate with them, the stronger we can craft our specific messaging and catch the attention of the people we can best serve on social media.

We can accordingly demonstrate how we can provide genuine help for our audience, demonstrate how we can offer solutions to their biggest problems, and the value they exchange in return is through purchasing the solutions we're offering.

This might sound a bit like sales, and truthfully, it is. People are absolutely more important than profits, but if no money ever gets exchanged, then we only have a glorified hobby instead of a business. However, packaging our value properly gets us past the uncomfortable "sales" part, and done right, they will even thank us for what we've provided. They may even provide feedback that helps us update our offers or create new ones. We'll touch more on this point shortly.

The more clearly we've defined our foundation, the easier it is to leverage social media to share exactly who we are and what we can offer. When we can offer value upfront, sharing who we really are with people rather than seeking a credit card every time they see us, the greater the loyalty you'll earn, and your customers will stick with you for life.

And that, my friend, is the real power of social media marketing.

GOLDEN RULE: Listen To Your Customers

There is a steady stream of conversation all day, every day on social media; some good, some bad, and ever present. If we want to be seen in a positive light, we are wise to be responsive on social media lest it goes the other way. We'll go deeper into this in Stage 5, but for now, it's enough to say that marketing well in business means we show up and listen for opportunities on social media for our brands.

For example, I was sitting in the car dealership waiting for my car to get some needed repair work completed. It was readily apparent that the people helping me didn't think customer service was a priority. More specifically, I felt that their body language, tone, and how they engaged me didn't match up to the "polite" words they were sharing with me. In short, it felt like they didn't much care that I was there.

Perhaps you've experienced something similar? To be blunt, it just leaves a bad taste in the mouth when this happens.

Annoyed and bored, I took to Twitter and mentioned the business and tweeted, "I am so frustrated. I wish this wasn't happening." Barely five minutes passed when someone tapped me on the shoulder and said, "Mrs. Heuman, we would love to speak with you."

I have to be honest, at first, it felt like I was getting called to the principal's office for a reprimand, but I was pleasantly surprised to find myself instead of sitting with a customer service representative who monitored the Twitter feed for the dealership. He began to ask me about my frustrations and went to work to provide me a solution. Just imagine my surprise when I saw that he offered me a much different (and far better) solution to what I had been offered just moments previously. It was a fantastic, first-hand demonstration of how paying attention to social media can be a huge benefit for a brand that's listening.

Hence, I strongly encourage you also to pay attention to your social media. More importantly, do you communicate with your audience so they know you're listening? The more they understand there's someone on your side of the screen as well, the more they will interact and help you grow your brand. As we've stated previously, all business is ultimately about people, and this is a fantastic way to be more connected.

GOLDEN RULE:
Be So Awesome People Shout It Everywhere On Social Media

One of the greatest benefits of providing excellent customer service is that people will talk about you even without you asking for it. Of course, many people are more likely to communicate a negative experience, but it's worth it to keep showing up to wow people and encourage the positives.

A lovely friend of mine, Shunta Grant, created the brand "Because of Zoe." She is an exceptional business coach, and her business continues to evolve into something even greater. The first time I met her was at a business conference where she was leveraging Instagram to make great connections with her customers. She has another business that creates these wonderful hair bows she sells in small boutique shops across the country. She also sells them through Instagram encouraged her customers to post pictures of their children wearing the bows after they received them.

It provides her plenty of content featuring these beautiful young girls with their locks of hair pulled back in the "Because of Zoe" bows. We'll cover more about content later, but for now, let's recognize the interactive nature of the exchanges that provide the chance to engage directly with her audience and provide excellent customer service. She could easily comment on all the lovely pictures that were shared across countless Instagram feeds, which let her reach a greater audience and create more brand awareness.

Being visible is one of the most important things you can do to increase your social media presence, help more people get to know and talk about you, and keep your business at the front of their minds. Note that these strategies can be applied to whichever platform you use. The important part is to create a positive experience for your audience, and they will gladly return the favor.

STAGE TWO

OPTIMIZE RELATIONSHIPS

The opportunity for you to build, cultivate, and nurture relationships can be life-changing for you and those you serve. When people like, know and truly trust what you are telling them, you can positively impact their decision to do business with you.

Our strong foundation laid, let's move into the next Golden Rule:

GOLDEN RULE:

It Isn't About Who You Know, Or What You Know, But About Who Knows You

This might seem obvious, but we're entering a phase where we're automating far too much with AI-based communications. Too many companies and marketers are trying to replace relationships with things like messenger bots, SEO, sales funnels, and gamification, and the effects are not good.

These can be helpful tools, but if we're trying to use them to replace relationships, we're making a huge mistake. Customers still want to be heard and understood. They want to know someone still cares about them instead of just feeling like a pawn in a business scheme designed to drain them of every last penny.

Now, more than ever, creating positive relationships will help you stand out from the crowd. The greater the relationship, the more they will spread the good word about you, and the greater your audience becomes.

In this stage, we're going to explore ways you can optimize these growing relationships on social media.

Being human and building relationships that show you care matters in business, and it definitely matters on social media.

Let's face it. Nobody looks forward to getting on the phone with their bank or insurance company and listening to automated voice messages. Oh, how I remember the days of needing to call my insurance company and using their voice activation prompts. But what they failed to realize (or take into consideration) is that I had a two-year-old in the background watching *Barney* or *Peppa Pig*, so each time I would try to tell them my social security number (plus an extra "Momma" in the background, the entire voice prompt would fail, and I'd have to start all over.

This is not the customer service I wanted, and it certainly wasn't helping me get the information I needed faster. It just left me feeling frustrated and on a mission to hit any number I could just so I could be heard by a human and get my issue resolved.

That isn't too much to ask for, is it?

And yet, as business owners, we hear some experts and trends saying that AI (automated intelligence) is the way of the future in social media marketing. I, on the other hand, with over eighteen years of digital and online marketing experience, can tell you that people are craving to be heard. Customers are seeking businesses and brands that will not only listen but respond in a timely manner. Customers want connection, and they want prompt service.

connection & prompt service!

"About 32% of all customers would stop doing business with a brand they loved after one bad experience."

On social media, when businesses show up and invest their marketing in such a way that gives value and helps make the audience smarter and better off than they were before they connected with you, then I believe businesses win, and the customers win.

Isn't that what we want? Improved business goals and happy clients? I'm hoping at this point that you are nodding your head in agreement. If so, that means we're both excited about using social media to positively impact your business while also honoring our customers in such a way that leaves a favorable impression on you.

Mark W. Schaefer, a globally recognized keynote speaker, educator, business consultant, and author said, "The best human company wins" in his book *Marketing Rebellion*. I agree 100 percent.

GOLDEN RULE:

Connection is the New Currency

Kelly Montgomery is the Owner/Operator of Kelzcuts Studio in Naperville, IL that I had the pleasure of getting to know as a member of Social Thrive Business Academy.

As a result of making videos and posting them on social media (that she did because of a video challenge in the Academy), her customer base increased. New clients were given an opportunity to see what she had to offer in a relaxed and informative manner. Her audience began to feel they knew her. They started feeling comfortable with her. And then, they began messaging her on Facebook and inquiring about her services.

At first, Kelly was nervous about putting herself out there on video. She felt the videos needed to be super polished and with a professional backdrop. That simply isn't the case. At first, Kelly was nervous on camera and didn't feel completely comfortable, but she kept making videos and posting them on Facebook anyway.

And guess what? She kept getting better. And more people started watching, and more connections were made. More people began responding to her videos by commenting and liking her posts. Kelly began not only feeling better about being on camera, but she actually started to enjoy it and started adding more and more of her personality in her videos. The results of creating and organizing her video content on social media helped Kelly realize she had a lot of pertinent information to share with her audience. Kelly says,

> "The engagement has been wonderful and has inspired a new way for my business to serve my customers. Focusing my attention and using certain platforms like Facebook and Instagram showed me I didn't need to spread myself in an ineffective manner and try to be everywhere. That made me enjoy using social media again. When you know better, you do better. I feel this rings true for me, and I'm having fun in the process!"

GET OUT OF YOUR OWN WAY

Business owners sometimes prohibit themselves from growing before they even get started on social media. Why? Sometimes it is negative self-talk that tells us that we need to look a certain way before we make the next video, or that the post we want to put out celebrating new product or services we have available will seem as if we're bragging.

Recently, I was talking with a business owner who has been in business for six years in South Carolina with a brick and mortar location. She felt that people would judge her or think, *Who does she think she is*, if she put a video or photo of their new mobile location. When I asked her why she thought that, she said, "I don't know. I just fear that it will seem as if I'm being boastful." Sure, there are people who show up on social media and don't balance the type of content they showcase, but that doesn't mean you can't show up the right way and showcase great things that are happening.

It is your job as a business owner and leader in your industry to believe that you have value. Your customers deserve to see you showing up ready to inspire them, motivate them, give them great offerings, and get to know you and your business. Social media is a fantastic distribution opportunity for you to do that.

You are responsible for the actions you take, so make sure that you aren't allowing yourself to be one of the biggest stumbling blocks in your marketing efforts.

Emotional connections increase business.

There is just one chance to make a first impression. And often, people are checking out businesses on social media before they even make it to their website. So. what does that mean for you and me?

It means that we have a great opportunity to not only show up on social media, consistently putting out our best content, but it also means we have many chances to build relationships that can help us stand apart from our competition.

Emotions are the driving force behind 50% of buying decisions. I don't know about you, but I think that is a very big number and definitely one that I want to pay attention to in running my business. Building an emotional connection with your audience allows for you to earn their trust, get noticed, resonate with them on a deeper level, and strengthens your connection. Here are some tips:

1. Create a Routine

Post on social media with a consistency that your audience can look forward to. If you post a quick tip each Tuesday at noon, before long, your audience will anticipate and look forward to your ritual. This will build an emotional connection with your brand. Plus, keeping you top of mind is always a business win.

2. Backstage Matters

What you think people don't want to see (or isn't important) is often exactly what you should post. Differentiate yourself from the competition by taking time to allow your audience to feel your excitement before your next speaking event or as you are doing a walk-through on a home closing.

3. Over-Deliver Because It Works

When you can say yes, and it doesn't even cost you money, it can be memorable. Say yes when it does cost you money, and you can blow people away. Rather than saying to yourself, *We can't do that for every customer*, tell yourself, *We can do it for this customer, and they'll remember us in a very favorable way because of it.* This can lead to happy customers going to social media to share their excitement.

4. Make Them Smarter, and You're the Champion

When you can enhance someone's day with information, services, products, or the latest video, you'll have your customers feeling like the hero, and you are what made them feel this way. That emotional connection will stick, and so will your brand when they need more of what you have to offer.

5. Have Empathy

One of the best ways you can let your audience know that you are human is to show up on social media with empathy and feeling. This could be over the loss of someone important within the business, unfortunate circumstances impacting a community, or a situation that comes to your attention via other media. When things are tugging on the hearts of your audience/community, consumers will remember you and notice that you put people as a top priority.

GOLDEN RULE:
Treat Others The Way You Want To Be Treated

We are a curious species. We're biologically wired for connection, yet we crave our technology to "advance" the world. If we take a closer look and what we're doing, we're creating tools to bring us closer together and then use them to keep us apart.

Think about it: when is the last time you called your utility or phone company and someone actually answered the phone? If they're using the technology correctly, the prompts should help us get to the right person, but what about the times we just keep getting pushed around in a circle before the system ultimately hangs up on us?

There's nothing wrong with using technology to enhance our relationships and communications, but we make a massive mistake when we use it to replace the human element. If you really want to stand out from your competition, amplify the humanity of your business, let people know they matter, treat them with honor and respect, and they will happily and more frequently talk about you. Bryan Kramer, the founder of H2H Marketing, drives this point constantly when he is leading well in the online marketing space. I like how Kramer states, "Let's humanize business. We envision technology and people working together to build stronger human connections." When you do this, your audience will grow like wildfire. And the best part? You're going to enjoy what you're doing even more.

In a time where we see trends of chatbots and AI (artificial intelligence) in marketing, there are so many things that might make us feel that going old school and talking to people is outdated. But the reality is that actually isn't the case. We as a culture are so inundated with the aggravation of automated recordings and robots when we call our insurance companies, banks, and customer service anywhere that we can't even get real people. We walk into a business and have staff look at us and say, "You need to go home and go online to get that accomplished."

People are frustrated, and I want you to know that the more humanity you bring to your business, the more people appreciate it. It will help you stand out in your business if you're not a cookie-cutter like everyone else. And when you apply these things on social media, it's going to make your business shine. I want you to know that I am a firm believer that relationships matter, that connections matter, and it strengthens your ability to stand out among other businesses. This is how you get your business to come up in conversation at the next backyard barbecue or professional event when someone in conversation mentions a topic or issue that is related to what you do.

Showing up, treating people the way that we want to be treated, and actually implementing the golden rule, truly is a game-changer. I remember hearing about the golden rule as a young child. In fact, right now, I can visualize the door of my kindergarten classroom in Georgetown, South Carolina, and a red poster showing the golden rule and treating others the way that you want to be treated. That's the premise of this entire book. My whole framework is talking about the gold of social media, and it's this concept of bringing together a framework of doing unto people the way that we would want to be done to us. The Golden Rule is the ethical principle of treating other people as one's self would prefer to be treated. In fact, here are just a few of the verses from the Bible:

> "So in everything, do to others what you would have them do to you, for this sums up the Law and the Prophets." Matthew 7:12

> "Do to others as you would have them do to you." Luke 6:31

So, who is Heather Heuman?" I'm a Jesus-centered, social media strategist, speaker, and host of the *Business, Jesus and Sweet Tea* podcast. I've helped hundreds of clients bring their powerful services and products into the marketplace via my private coaching and social media marketing services. In my signature offer, Social Thrive Business Academy, I bring years of business and marketing experience to my students so that they can create relationship-building social media content that draws ideal clients in like strawberry jam on a buttermilk biscuit.

I'm also a wife, mom of three, global speaker, and business owner who has not only helped others grow their businesses with social media, but I do it all on the back of having built two businesses over the last eight years to beyond six figures each.

It might make some people uncomfortable that my personal take on business is rooted in Christianity, and that's okay. Please take a closer look at the underlying principle, and you'll realize the premise of this entire book is based on the ultimate golden rule: treat people as they wish to be treated. However, doesn't it just make sense that we take care of each other?

The greater point is that combining an attitude of serving others with social media marketing will plant the seeds of growth that will serve both you and your audience for years to come. We can further the purpose of bettering humanity to be blunt, I believe that is our responsibility as business owners, whether Christian or otherwise. It's been a joy and a privilege to use my gifts and talents over the past nineteen years in online marketing, and the relationships I have gained over that time are priceless. You can have the same, and the principles shared in this book will help you get there.

It's worth it to show up authentically, invest the time and energy into others, and to leverage social media to advance your efforts. The rewards go well beyond just the financial and can enrich the lives of both you and your audience.

GOLDEN RULE:
Go Where Your People Already Spend Time On Social Media

It sure feels like everyone is on social media, but is that an exaggeration? Maybe not: according to research in 2019 by Statista.com, 79% of the US population has a social media profile, and 2.34 *billion* people worldwide are on social media. In other words, the odds are pretty good your desired audience is already there and waiting for you.

For example, when I started my first business ElizabethtownFamily.com in 2011, I focused most of my social media efforts on Facebook as that's where my audience was already spending much of their time.

I scoured online and local offline resources for affordable, family-friendly activities local to Fort Knox, Kentucky, and posted them to a Facebook page as I continued working on the website. Facebook's tools allowed me to narrow my focus to my target audience, which is busy moms aged 20 to 45 years old living within a 30-mile radius of the community.

It was so exciting when I go the first "like." (Thanks, Mom!) Of course, I told my friends how I had created the business, and they told their friends as well. It began growing organically from there, and the completed website was ready three months later. I included the Facebook audience as part of the traffic to the new website, where I was further able to expand and began growing my email list.

MOVE IN THE MESSY

Many business owners are fearful of getting started in the midst of the messy. My own launch might not have been ideal, but they don't have to be so long as we get into motion. No matter where we begin, we're still going to grow and improve. Far better to just get started rather than waiting for the perfection we're not likely to ever experience this side of heaven.

POWER OF COMMUNITY ON FACEBOOK

Pamela Skyberg Digby is a dear woman I met while I was speaking in Dallas, Texas, in the fall of 2018. She is a kind yet soft-spoken woman who came up to me after my talk to share with me how much she enjoyed it. She shared with me a piece of her own journey using Facebook to have community and how much it meant to her son, Jared, who had a lethal genetic disorder called Ataxia-Telangiectasia (A-T). This awful disease attacks children, causing progressive loss of muscle control, compromised immune systems, and a strikingly high rate of cancer, especially lymphoma and leukemia. Children with A-T are usually confined to wheelchairs by age ten and often do not survive their teens

Pamela's son Jared loved Facebook. They found a page and a private group to connect people affected by the disease, both of which she eventually led. Facebook gave them a safe space to talk about their journey, stories, and experiences they shared on a similar path. Pamela and Jared found and gave love in the Facebook page and Facebook group where they established community, friends that felt like family and created bonds with people they otherwise never would have found. Some of these people they never met in person, yet they had adoration and true friendship that felt like they had.

On April 29, 2012, Jared went to be with Jesus, but Jared left a magnificent legacy impact using the power of Facebook. Pamela wrote:

> "Facebook was my son Jared's only connection to the world. Thanks to him, it is also my connection to the world. It allows me to give of my time. It allows me to reach out to someone searching. It allows me to rejoice when someone is overcoming or achieving. It allows me to pray when someone needs prayer. It allows me to hurt with someone hurting and to cry with someone who is crying. It allows me to love and be loved. It allows me to be a light in the darkness. It allows me to shine for Jesus. It allows me a place to have continued purpose. My mission."

WHEN YOU ADD AWESOME INTO YOUR SOCIAL MEDIA GREATNESS HAPPENS

Mary Lu Saylor of Grow Real Companies sat in my living room in the summer of 2018, along with three other amazing businesswomen. It was Roshanda Pratt, Jennifer Bennett, and me, and we were so excited to be getting together for a great evening of food, fellowship, and marketing chatter. We were all friends who had connected on social media, but it was the first time I met Mary Lu face to face. As you can imagine, I felt as if I knew her and had even more connection with her after spending an evening laughing, building community, and getting to know one another a little more.

After a few months, Mary Lu joined my Social Thrive Business Academy, and I had the pleasure of seeing her business bloom upon the success she had already created. As a social media strategist, Mary Lu gets that when you put information out on social media for business or non-profit reasons, great things can happen.

During a video challenge inside Social Thrive, a former pastor friend of Mary Lu's saw one of the videos on LinkedIn she had created, and he emailed asking to meet to learn more about what her services were for helping non-profits.

After five minutes with Dr. Terry Lanford from Entrusted To Teach Ministries, Mary Lu knew that God was working on something very special. Mary Lu immediately started helping Entrusted to Teach Ministries to create visual content with videos and graphics that could help get the organization's message and upcoming events more visibility by leveraging Facebook. The win here is that they didn't just create one graphic and post it fourteen times until the event took place, a mistake many businesses and non-profits make.

Here are some specific takeaways you can learn from Mary Lu's use of great content to grow the ministry on Facebook:

1. Identify exactly who your audience is who you want to see your content.
2. Create visual content (video, graphics, and photos) telling a story about the specific message of the organization and upcoming events.
3. After posting the content on Facebook, pay attention to posts that get more engagement and reach than others and consider putting some Facebook advertising dollars behind posts doing well organically to increase getting the message into more of the right people's feed. $1 to $4 a day can really help. Start small if you want and pay attention to the results you start to get.

Mary Lu immediately started seeing more people coming to their Facebook page. They began getting more likes, comments, shares, and likes, and the page began to grow immediately. Some of you might think this is crazy, but Mary Lu did this free of charge because she felt convicted by God that it what she was supposed to do.

After the event, Dr. Lanford hired Mary Lu to manage the Entrusted To Teach Facebook page. She has formed a strong partnership where she meets and discusses overall marketing ideas, not just social media. Because Mary Lu has a plethora of experience, she has been able to use her television background to help with promotion ideas and reach out to contacts to have Dr. Lanford of Entrusted To Teach interviewed. He regularly shares stories with Mary Lu about people who comment on the Facebook page about how informative and creative his page is, which has led to more donations to his ministry. Part of his ministry is teaching different types of classes that churches need to thrive and survive, and Dr. Lanford always mentions Mary Lu and her business.

Mary Lu is very excited by how social media has helped her have work opportunities beyond her wildest expectations and helping her clients the wins they need. After being patient—which you and I know is not always easy—Mary Lu continues to follow God's direction for her business.

WHY FACEBOOK GROUPS AND LINKEDIN GROUPS

As demonstrated, the power of community is very strong in groups on both Facebook and LinkedIn. People crave connection with others who share common interests, skill sets, trials, and needs. This is why social media groups can be so powerful in helping you find new people that can use what your business has to offer. They can also foster connection with others to nurture experiences and with whom you can collaborate. In short, they offer a fine opportunity to expand your network.

Best Practices in Groups on Social Media

1. **Don't Spam** - It's off-putting, doesn't come across very genuine, and makes for a lousy first impression even if you really are the best in the business at what you do. Odds are good the admins will give you the boot if you spam anyway, so why take the chance?
2. **Give Value** – Remember that groups exist to exchange value, not just take. You'll gain a following as you answer the questions you can while getting answers to your own. It might sound odd, but the less you expect in return, the more you're likely to get.
3. **Be Kind** – Isn't the world already challenging enough to navigate? We all have so much pressure on us to perform and can drown in a constant sea of noise with others screaming their various messages that it can get quite overwhelming. It's the ones with a kind and encouraging word that stand out and make the best impressions.
4. **Consistently Engage** – People also appreciate regular contact. We experience enough chaos in life that some stability can go a long way. From a strategic standpoint, your consistency will help you get noticed. Consider creating a scheduled routine so you can regularly engage with groups that are of importance to you. In turn, you will become more familiar to others, and they will seek you out as an authority on your topic, which will then lead to more business opportunities.

GOLDEN RULE:
Be the Best Human

My direct connection to Mark Schaefer came about as a result of a Twitter exchange while attending Social Media Marketing World in 2015. We had connected online a few months before that and finally had the chance to connect in person. Previously, he was just someone I respected on social media for his content and didn't fully expect just how great an impact meeting him would have to this day on my business.

Had I just made a connection, taken a selfie (of course) and walked away, that would have been lovely; it's what most people do, but I didn't stop there. I continued to engage with his content on social media, and later that December, I included him on a short list of people who had made a significant impact on me. I used some simple graphics to create a canvas print and mailed it to him as a Christmas gift. Imagine my excitement when his thank you note arrived in my email a short time later!

There were two reasons behind that gift. First, he genuinely made an impact on me, and I wanted to share my appreciation for him. Sharing our kindness with others goes a long way in this world, and I love to keep that gratitude in motion.

Second, it was also a strategic move to stay on his radar. He speaks to countless thousands of people around the world at various conferences, but how many of them do you suppose sent him a Christmas gift? How many people do you suppose maintain that connection with follow-ups and consistently sharing their content over time? It's these small things that can make a profound difference in our relationships and help us grow over time.

About a year later, I was feeling stuck in business. Something was off about my business model, and I was hoping for Mark's opinion. I sent him an email wondering if he could answer a quick question about my situation and how he might handle it if he were in my shoes. I was pleasantly surprised when his response came less than five minutes later wondering if I wanted to get on the phone with him the following Monday. Which, of course, I did, and we traded phone numbers.

(Quick Tip: If you ever get a Facebook message, an email, a direct message on Instagram, or a message on LinkedIn or any communication, you can often get quick responses if you promptly write them back while they may still be online.)

I nervously dialed the phone on that Monday and was warmly greeted by this brilliant man who doesn't often make such arrangements on account of his rather busy schedule for which he gets paid very well. I had narrowed down my questions to three specifics in order to respect his time. Yet, more than an hour passed before we wrapped up, and I will forever sing his praises for his generosity. His suggestions have influenced my business to this day and looking back at the entire scenario, it all came about as a result of one single tweet.

Hence, it's worth it to be a good human being on social media just as we should be in "real" life. We can affect people we haven't met in person and influence their lives for the better. What began as a business relationship with Mark has turned into a valued friendship that afforded me the pleasure of him saying yes to write the foreword for this book, and you will undoubtedly experience the same as you continue to grow your own business.

The next time you're thinking that social media can't move the needle in your business, take courage and set that thought aside. Let go of that small thinking and look at the bigger picture of what's actually available to you. Just as strong ropes are formed from the smallest threads, so are the relationships you can build when using social media to its greatest potential. Just be real with people, and they'll do the same for you.

GOLDEN RULE:
Use Your Best Online Etiquette

I joined a handful of guests on a Facebook Live for a wonderful conversation when it was still a new feature. Mentioning that I had some clients in the pet and grooming industry led me to connect with Bella Vasta, who I enjoyed getting to know and building a stronger connection.

She was watching that Facebook Live and simply made a comment that turned into a direct message conversation and then a phone conversation. It turned out we had some great mutual connections regarding the content that we worked with in the marketing space. We eventually interviewed each other on our podcasts, and it grew beyond a working relationship. It's how we ultimately became friends, and it was born of a simple comment on a Facebook Live. I could have ignored it, but I'm sure glad I didn't. It's another fine example of how we can use social media to connect with others.

A word of warning: Don't be "that" person. You know the one we're talking about. The type who shows up in a group and spouts off how they have the solution to all of your problems. Or the one who reaches out asking you for sales and other such things without even getting to know you. Or they just want to do you a favor and then immediately ask for your 5-star review. Or maybe they're the one asking for the favor, and they'll catch you on the next round only to disappear as soon as the task is done.

You know. *That* person. Please, please, please don't ever be that person. Don't even let the thought enter your mind.

Everything we've covered is designed to help you optimize your presence and relationships through social media. As we've stated before, it's incredibly powerful when used properly, and the following guidelines can help achieve that end.

1) Tagging people genuinely in your posts. This is perhaps among the easiest ways to engage other users. It is to show up on social media focused only on your business and content but tagging others can increase the chance they will join the conversation and interact with you.

This doesn't mean we tag dozens of people or more at a time. That would be a form of spam, and at least as of this writing, most social media platforms are cracking down on this practice with Facebook leading the charge.

That stated, it is quite reasonable to tag a few people related to your post, even if we're not directly connected to them. For example, let's say you're creating a post that spotlights Tony Robbins. It makes sense to tag him, particularly if what you're sharing will resonate with his audience as well as yours. Doing so will significantly increase the number of people who will see your post, which can further expand your audience. This is the type of activity social media platforms encourage and will even help you when you interact with those that like, follow, or comment on what you've shared, giving you the possibility of further expanding your audience.

In short, tag wisely and strategically.

2) Not all social activity happens in your personal feed. As business owners, we can often feel we're wearing too many hats. For all we have to do to keep business moving forward, there is a temptation to count our scheduled posts on social media for the week and think we're done. However, it's a good idea to check other people's feeds to see what's going on in their world and interact with them as well.

This will help you get a feel for what's going on in your audience's lives and offer more opportunities to network. Say, for example, someone you follow is hosting an event, and it could lead to a chance to work together. You can easily share what they're doing with your audience to help them gain greater awareness, which benefits both you and the person you're helping promote.

3) Nurture the relationships you create through consistency. It goes a long way with people when you consistently show up. Part of the reason Bella and I were able to build such a connection is that we chose to regularly interact with one another both professionally and personally before we started working together. It doesn't have to be anything fancy: just say hi or comment on their content when you're online, particularly with those you want to work with.

4) Celebrate others on social media. Yes, we need to get business done, but we don't have to be all serious all the time and when someone hits a milestone or gets a win, celebrate with them! Letting others know you care about them, that it's not all about you or the next sale helps you be seen as the leader you really are. We all enjoy being recognized for our wins and creates positive motivation for everyone. This could be as simple as clicking the share button on Facebook when you see a fellow friend, colleague, or business owner win an award or have a cause for celebration.

5) Personalization wins every time. Particularly when we're making new connections on social media, make sure you personalize your messages. None of us like the cut and paste messages that plague our inboxes and feels more like spam.

This doesn't mean you have to write long messages. Instead, you can highlight things you have in common like maybe you work in the same niche or share a common hobby. This helps you and your new contact break the ice, get the dialogue started, and helps them know you're taking the time to be interested in them personally rather than just your next sales target.

6) Introverts and extroverts. There are plenty of business owners that call themselves introverts. They prefer the online marketing space because it's them in their pajamas and their computer to keep minimal connections with people face-to-face. I myself am pretty introverted, yet I love connecting with people.

I share this to let you know that social media is a great way for you to create relationships both online and offline, regardless of your personality type. Social media can help you nurture your relationships. However, it's up to you to decide to communicate with people strictly online or eventually meet in person. I encourage you to consider meeting more people in person as it does help to make you more relatable, but you can do it at your pace and when you're ready.

Meeting people in person can be as simple as a dinner meeting with a few people or maybe a networking event. You don't have to be the life of the party when you get there, but it does help to optimize those relationships. Wherever you end up, it's worth it to pull out your phone and check-in (on Facebook, for example) at the event where you are and take a few photos while you're there.

You don't have to post in real-time if you don't want to, and we'll talk more about what to do with the footage in another chapter.

GOLDEN RULE:
Know How to Handle your Haters the Right Way

I remember sitting there talking to my client as he was furious about a review he had received on Facebook. It was not a review that anyone of us would want. In fact, it was one that showcased how someone who had hired him for his services was displeased. However, this was not a typical negative review where someone put a one or two-sentence comment that they were frustrated. The customer had complained in length over two paragraphs about how he felt frustrated about his experience using the client's service. The business owner felt wrongfully accused and was ready to lash out because he had a very different perspective on the situation.

Have you ever felt that way?

Have you ever felt that you wanted to lash out at someone who was saying untrue things about your business? Let's talk about how to handle haters with grace and kindness in this specific situation. This particular client, who was fairly active in engaging on their own social platform, hired our team to help them create new content and strategy to align with their business goals, and we were consulting with them and sharing best practices.

Even though I gave my best suggestion, which I'm going to share with you in just a moment, my client did the exact opposite. He went to Facebook and not only responded to the client (which is not a bad thing), but he responded with probably a three or four-paragraph message going into great detail about both the person who had responded, their spouse, and—you know, you can imagine the rest. It was not very pretty. I sunk my head and sat there in disbelief saying, *Is this really what's happening?* I'm here to tell you, I get it. It is absolutely frustrating when you feel someone on social media is not showcasing your truth.

TIPS FOR HANDLING YOUR HATERS ON SOCIAL MEDIA

1. Get the conversation offline as quickly as possible. If you receive negative feedback, acknowledge that you see their post with a very short and simple comment. An example in the situation above would be something like, "We're sorry to hear about your recent experience. Someone from our team will be reaching out to you." This is important because it lets other people see you are addressing the situation.

2. Do not get into a back-and-forth battle of the words. After you reply once on social media, make every effort possible to end the public conversation and get the dialogue either on the phone, via e-mail, or face-to-face if necessary.

3. Remember we're all human. We all have hard days, and unfortunately, those may be days where people lash out on social media more so than they might if their personal day were going differently.

4. Integrity wins, so take the high road. This doesn't mean that whatever the customer says is true. It just means that you alone are responsible for the way you conduct yourself, and you need to remember that social media is public, and people will read the comments.

5. Block and delete may be necessary. Depending on the social media platform, there may be the option to delete, ban, or block. If someone is profane or completely offensive in their word choices or language, it may be best just to choose to remove their comments completely or block them from your page.

6. Facebook Reviews are extremely difficult to remove once they have been posted to your page. You do have the option to request from Facebook that they be removed, but in my six years of working directly with clients for social media marketing, not once has Facebook deleted a negative review, no matter the circumstances.

STAGE THREE

CHOOSE THE RIGHT PLATFORMS

YOU DON'T NEED TO BE A SLAVE TO SOCIAL MEDIA

We absolutely want to leverage social media, but we don't want to become a slave to it. There are so many platforms available, and it might seem a good idea to try to be on all of them to maximize our reach, but this is not the case. If we try to stretch ourselves too thin into too many areas, all of them will suffer, and we'll get the opposite effect.

The platforms we choose might be free, but social media does cost time and money. When we first start out, we will likely have more time than money to invest, which is where the temptation to spread ourselves out often comes from.

Say, for example, you have two hours you can commit each week to social media. How effective do you suppose you could be with that time trying to spread yourself on five platforms as opposed to one or two? I actually encourage my clients to concentrate at least 80-85% of their social media time to one ideal platform and at most play a bit with a second. This helps avoid feeling like social media is taking over your life and leaving you emotionally drained.

The truth is that we do not need to be on all the platforms, particularly at the beginning of our journey in business on social media. This is also true if your business has been around for years, yet you are new to using social media. Concentrating on one (or possibly two) is a far better strategy for using your time effectively, making first impressions, and avoiding overwhelm.

As you grow your business, you can start outsourcing parts of your social media and consider expanding, but even then, we must be careful as we want to give our businesses the best chance to make a first impression.

THE KEY ELEMENTS TO PICKING A SOCIAL MEDIA PLATFORM

There are many factors to consider when making your decision on which social media platform to use. It's among the key reasons we covered who your audience is in the previous chapter as each platform operates differently, reaches a different audience, and serve a different purpose. This helps answer the two key questions we must ask when picking our social media platforms.

First, where does our audience spend most of their time? The more we understand the psychology and habits of the people we're trying to reach, the easier it will fit the pattern of what they're looking for on social media. This will greatly enhance our chances for success in connecting with our ideal audience.

Note that this a very different question of where we'd like them to be. We're going to have a much easier time gaining attention connecting with people where they're at rather than attempting to create a new audience where they're not.

This is another reason having a deep understanding of our audience is so helpful; knowing their behaviors and attitudes makes it so much easier to know where they're going to be so we can match our efforts to where they already are.

Second, what are your goals for being on social media? The possibilities are nearly endless and knowing what you want before starting will help you create the greatest possible impact for you and your audience. This will also help determine where to focus your time and energy in order to educate people best about your products and your services.

For example, if you're looking to generate business-to-business leads, LinkedIn is far more likely to be of use than Instagram. Or if perhaps you're looking for brides-to-be for your wedding planning service, Pinterest could be more useful than Twitter.

Third, take into consideration your strengths, the personality of you or your team, and your brand. This may not seem important but remember that building a presence on social media takes time, effort, and resources. You are going to be far more effective on a social platform that you enjoy rather than just gritting your teeth to get it done rather than enjoying it. Each platform is nuanced enough that trying to post somewhere we don't want to be is going to be reflected. Given that social media is where we're going to be the most exposed, it just makes sense to post where we can best express ourselves.

There are enough social media platforms available that you can find your ideal audience in a place you enjoy spending time, and we'll cover a few shortly. In the meantime, it's exciting to know we've reached an age in marketing in which we can focus on a very specific audience and still reach our end goals instead of trying to sell our wares to every last being we can.

GOLDEN RULE: Don't Say It and Spray It

If you're thinking about creating a single piece of content and spreading the same copy and the same image on every possible platform you can get your hands on—stop! There's a strong temptation to do this for the time it can potentially save, particularly for tools that can automatically post for us in numerous locations, but there are some serious hazards to this approach.

Let's take Blue Cross Blue Shield of South Carolina for an example. Ryal Curtis, the Senior Social Media Strategist at Blue Cross, is leading the way with innovation and let's be real, here—it's health insurance. Yet, he spearheads a dynamic team that has created a fun, trendy, exciting campaign. They have figured out how to get people talking about health, the purpose of having goals, and how to live fearlessly. They work with the Columbia Fireflies, a minor league baseball team, and regularly encourage people to be more fit. This all ties in with their content program in which they regularly share useful content like health tips and amazing recipes like zucchini banana cake with cream frosting. Yum! I even love the custom hashtag they use: #LiveFearlessSC.

Most importantly, they connect with their customers and employees alike, demonstrating the benefits of good health, which all relates to their core business in a positive way. We could paraphrase their message as "We're here to help you take care of yourself from start to finish" and use Facebook perfectly to share what they stand for.

If we were to examine their Twitter feed, it delivers shorter messages in a more news-flavored variety because that's what the platform is better designed for. The content may have the same core messaging but is delivered to fit the platform rather than just trying to duplicate the same content in both places. Remember that the culture of each platform is going to be different, and we are wise to create custom content with custom graphics or video that fits each platform.

It's worth repeating that we should focus and optimize 80–85% of our social media efforts on one platform. If we're going to use a second platform, tweak the content to match the culture, and strongly consider scheduling what you share there for at least a few days separate from your first platform.

If you're still worried about any of this, consider this:

If a health insurance company can make social media look fresh, exciting, and approachable, the rest of us are in great shape to do the same.

WHERE SHOULD YOU BE TO FIND YOUR CUSTOMERS

We covered the key elements of picking a social media platform. As a specialist in social media, the five platforms I believe to be of the greatest value are LinkedIn, Facebook, Instagram, Twitter, and Pinterest. I use the first four in my business on a regular basis to stay in contact with and expand my customer base as well as grow my email list with new prospects. Even though Pinterest is amazing, it isn't the right fit for my business, so I don't use it very much. However, we will cover that platform as well. Please also keep in mind that I have a team who helps me maintain my presence on four platforms, and I still recommend you master one platform before expanding to another.

Perhaps you're already on one or more of these platforms and if so, ask yourself if you're spending 70% or more of your time there. If your audience is already there, then you're already in good shape! Otherwise, you might want to consider shifting your time and efforts to match your audience better.

Before we dive into some numbers, go to Google, and type in the name of your business. Google indexes your social media pages, which can provide extra insight into where to focus your time and energy. This is valid whether you have an online or local business, and it's worth your time to make sure your website is properly indexed with Google. Doing so will make your social media efforts that much more powerful across the platforms you use as well as on Google.

LinkedIn Statistics

- 9 billion content impressions on LinkedIn feeds every week
- 50% of Americans with college degrees use LinkedIn
- 80% of business-to-business leads come from LinkedIn
- 94% of B2B marketers use LinkedIn to distribute content
- 57% of LinkedIn users are on mobile

LinkedIn's reputation started off as a confusing platform where people would post resumes when they get out of college in the pursuit of a job. One can still do that to an extent, but LinkedIn has flourished into an exceptional networking platform that increasingly connects professionals and business owners through conversations and shared content. Their search options allow you to expand your network through simple searches easily.

They also provide groups to connect with others on common topics ranging anywhere from small business owners, hairstylists, realtors, mortgage brokers, and just about any other topic you can think of. Company pages are also easy to set up, though it's wise to get your personal LinkedIn profile up and running first.

Facebook Statistics

- 35% of Facebook ad audience is under 25
- The number of American Facebook users aged 65+ has grown from 20% (in 2012) to 41% (in 2018)
- 60% of Americans use Facebook
- 2.4 billion people log into Facebook every single month
- 50% of American teens use Facebook
- Roughly 210 million users are American, which is roughly 10% of all Facebook users
- 66% of monthly Facebook users are on Facebook every single day
- Americans spend 58 minutes per day on Facebook
- 88% of Facebook users are accessing Facebook via a mobile device
- 200 million people are members of meaningful Facebook groups
- 43% of Americans get their news from Facebook

- Facebook has over 80 million small-to-medium-sized business pages
- Facebook is the top platform for both B2B and B2C businesses

It's safe to say that Facebook defined much of what social media is today. Like many others, it has been a significant part of my adult life. I'm 44 years old at the time of writing this, and I have been on there since I was around 32. My kids were young, and like most others, I started using it to post photos so my family far away could readily see them. Few of us logged into Facebook the first time for the purpose of business, but the ability to share our memories can make a timeline a positive, enjoyable experience, particularly since we can connect with others far away that we might not otherwise stay in touch.

Even though the audience is so massive and readily accessible, keep in mind how most of us use Facebook to keep in personal touch rather than looking for businesses to advertise to us. If we're to engage people on this platform, we must be showing up with relevant, compelling information if we're to get people to stop scrolling and join us in a conversation.

Make a thorough study of your data and statistic regarding your audience before overly committing your time to Facebook. You may very well find your audience here, but people on this platform aren't necessarily looking to be marketed to.

Twitter Statistics

- 321 million monthly active users are on Twitter
- 80% of Twitter users are on mobile
- 46% of those people are on the platform every day
- 70% of Twitter users say they use the network to get their news
- 42% of Twitter users are between the ages of 30 to 64

- 93% of people who follow small and medium-sized businesses on Twitter plan to purchase from brands they follow according to a survey
- 69% have already purchased from a small business because of something that they saw on Twitter

Twitter is best known for real-time engagement. Some even refer to it as micro-blogging, meaning you take the thoughts that you have, what's going on in your business, what's happening in life and condense it to a maximum of 280 characters. This is twice the original 140 characters, though statistics show that shorter messages general outperform longer messages. Popular in the sports industry and traditional media, it's a great place to make connections with influencers with whom might not otherwise be able to connect and get the latest and breaking news around the world. Personally, it's helped me make many wonderful connections, grow my business, and nurture relationships with people with whom I would otherwise never have had a chance to get past their gatekeeper.

Instagram Statistics

- 1 billion monthly active users
- 500 million daily active users
- 400 million daily Instagram stories users
- 59% of U.S. users are under 60
- 60% of Instagram users that visit the site each day
- 35% of U.S. adults in 2018 use Instagram (up from 28% in 2016)

Instagram is a great platform for visual appearance and can support both photos and short videos. Make sure you post the highest possible quality to stand out from the crowd, which we will explore further later in the book.

Pinterest Statistics

- 291 million monthly (1/3 are from the United States)
- 40% of new signups are men (a 70% increase over a one-year period)
- 35% have an income of over $75,000
- 34% of users reside in the suburbs
- Travelers are 2x more likely to use Pinterest
- 30% of users reside in urban areas
- 50% of millennials use Pinterest every day
- 25% of users reside in rural areas
- The average time spent on Pinterest is 14.2 minutes
- 93% of users use Pinterest to make purchasing decisions
- 55% of U.S. online shoppers suggest Pinterest is their favorite online platform
- 80% of all Pinterest searches happen on mobile

Please take note that people are increasingly turning to social media to search, research, plan their purchases, and are increasingly using mobile devices to do it. Keep that in mind as you're optimizing the appearance of your content.

These statistics should help you better identify where you should be on social media to meet your ideal audience. I caution you again against trying to be too many platforms at once as they all function very differently to suit their unique cultures.

Further, these statistics are current as of this writing and will likely shift in the future. If we count Facebook as the game-changing platform for social media, we're not even fifteen years into this highly dynamic environment. You don't need to devote massive amounts of time to studying trends, but it is worth keeping tabs on where the changes are happening so you can more readily adapt to them as they come.

We've covered the very basics of each platform, and inside my community, Social Thrive Business Academy, we go much deeper into the nuts and the bolts of the platforms we just reviewed. We cover exact strategies to create content plans and execute them, and which platforms can best match your goals, right down to the exact buttons you need to push to make it all come together. You can find more information by visiting www.joinsocialthrive.com if that feels like the help you are looking for.

Let's next dive into content.

STAGE FOUR

INFLUENTIAL CONTENT

We've established a strong foundation for our business, our identity, our ideal audience, what they need, and what we can offer them. We agree that optimizing relationships is imperative on social media, and the ones we have are the perfect place for us to start. As we nurture those relationships, we can continue to create and cultivate a larger audience from there. By limiting the platforms we use, it's easier to show up authentically, and we can further our relationships from there.

The next step (and possibly the most important) is creating influential content. Not just information that can be seen elsewhere, but useful data, information, photos, and content that demonstrates you are an influencer. Content that establishes you have helped people get results and you have space in your calendar to help more customers. Getting this piece right on social media establishes credibility and shows people you can be trusted, and they'll recognize you as the real deal. In turn, they'll share and engage with your content, even if they haven't read it all, and help you grow your audience for you.

GOLDEN RULE:
Always Ask Yourself, "What's In It For Them" (the customer)

Blue Rooster of Blythewood is a small, quaint restaurant that opened its doors for customers March 2019. When they first opened, they were only open for lunch, and their sole means of marketing their business was a Facebook business page. I had the pleasure of meeting owner Trish Truesdale a few months prior after she told me she found me on Google and liked everything she saw about my company. And one of her first questions was, "How can you help me?" Quite a logical question, wouldn't you agree?

I told her nobody had a clue about her new business was, and that I could help her leverage social media to get visibility among the ideal customers she wanted and that we could address the pain points of her audience. In short, they were hungry, and she had great food.

Just like Trish asked me how I could help her, we need to always keep this in mind when we develop our social media content. After we created her new Facebook business page, we began filling it with great information, letting the community know about the menu items we'd be serving, and we created anticipation weeks before the restaurant was even open.

By consistently showing up each day with what her Blue Rooster Special is, customers know to check her Facebook page each day between 9:00 and 10:00 a.m. because she posts there first each day. We've had great fun showcasing pictures of the food, videos of the restaurant, testimonials of happy customers, and a roll-out of a Friday Night Fish Fry. Over the course of the first six months, Trish has been able to expand her customer base considerably by the power of social media.

In fact, their small Facebook page has grown from following from 0 to 1,000 likes in just a few months organically in

Blythewood that has a population of around 4,000 people. And the engagement on the page is through the roof with five times the people that follow the page. One of the best takeaways I could ask you to get out of this book is always to be asking yourself, "What's in it for them?" as you create content for social media.

Remember this golden rule, always.

GOLDEN RULE:
Your Voice Can Influence No Matter The Number Of Followers You Have

This doesn't mean we show all day long the most profound things we can think of. Sometimes, a humorous story can go much further than the deepest philosophical thought. More importantly, it's about showing exactly as you are, being honest with yourself and your audience, and doing so consistently.

Your authenticity and honesty are what will help you get noticed, grow your audience the right way, and help you develop the leads, sales, and brand awareness you want for your business. Personally, it has led me to amazing clients like Chick-fil-A, numerous chambers of commerce, churches, a variety of personal brands, business owners, and business brands, community organizations, and many others. I've helped my clients do the same for their own business, and it works every time.

As you create your content, think of your core messaging and how it best serves your audience. This is how to attract more of the right people as they will feel you are talking *with* them as opposed to *at* them, and they will be far more likely to call upon you when they need your services.

NEED CONTENT IDEAS HELP? If you are following along but would like some clear, direct, and practical content ideas, I have a free 31-day social media content calendar that you can go and get right now:

Snag the 31-day social media content calendar: Sweettea socialmarketing.com/contentcalendar

YOUR CONTENT VERSUS SHARING

We've all got that one friend on Facebook who shares at least forty things a day. Newsfeeds filled with quizzes, news clips, memes, and pictures of their dinner, forcing us to either scroll for a while to find anything personal or just abandon the search altogether.

It's as if they don't have a voice and have nothing to say themselves. It's just more noise cluttering up an already crowded space, and how often do we really engage with content like that? The point is that showing up with your own unique voice instead of simply sharing everyone else's content can be a real game-changer for you and your business.

First of all, it's going to let people see your business: what you're actually about, your thoughts, and your ideas. This is how you can showcase your personality or how your brand has decided to do business. Think of some of the brands we most like to follow that have created their own unique voice be they humorous, encouraging, and motivating, or any other combination of factors that hold our attention. They often offer us behind the scenes glimpses to demonstrate humanity in their business and become much more relatable in the process.

There might be a temptation to speak controversially to gain attention, and this is coached in some circles. Certainly, you can do that, but keep in mind that the loudest person is not always the smartest. For comparison, Chihuahuas sure know how to get attention, but they also have a reputation for a reason. In short, be careful about how you choose to employ this strategy.

That stated, it's well worth it to be yourself on social media. Trying to fake a personality isn't going to last for any length of time as you will eventually be uncovered for who we really are. Whether you're an introvert or an extravert, have a dry sense of humor or prefer puns, go with it. Remember we're in this for the long haul, and it will serve you and your audience so much better to show up exactly as you are.

If you're still not sure what to post, try this:

What are the top ten questions you get asked by your customers? If you don't yet have a big enough audience, what are the top ten questions your desired audience asks about your chosen topic? Google can help you determine these if you're not sure.

With this list, you can now create ten posts on social media. Simply create a post for each of the questions and making it stand-alone content. For example, if I hear my customers telling me that time on social media is their biggest frustration, I might make a post sharing my biggest advice for a business owner who struggles with time and getting around to doing their social media. Don't worry about what your competition is doing; create your posts and be sure to reflect your own personality as you do. Getting in the creative mode will unlock more ideas, and your content will become a natural extension of who you are and what you're thinking. Stay consistent with it and provide information your audience can use, and it will certainly grow.

GOLDEN RULE:
Encourage User-Generated Content

I've had business owners tell me there is no engagement happening on their social media feed, that nobody is posting or responding to their posts. Truthfully, it can sometimes take a while to cultivate an atmosphere that encourages people to engage. Remember that social media is a long-term play rather than a sprint, and your consistency will pay off in the long run.

This doesn't mean creating engaging content has to be complicated or difficult. Customers enjoy being recognized, and there are some easy ways to do this.

Take my clients at Hollow Creek Distillery in Leesville, South Carolina for example and their recently created brands High Cotton Bourbon and White Hot Cinnamon Whiskey. Not only do they take photos at their distillery when customers come in for tours, samples, and purchases, but they also encourage them to check-in on social media, post pictures, and make comments about their experiences with the new drink.

It helps develop extensive brand awareness, and more exposure to a larger audience than the distillery could otherwise reach on their own (some posts reached 13,000 with zero ad spend on Facebook even though they had less than 500 likes), and honestly, it's fun for everyone involved. The distillery can then share some of the more popular posts to the main newsfeed of the High Cotton Bourbon Facebook page, which builds more credibility and it keeps growing from there.

Allowing your customers to be part of your marketing strategy on social media is a wise move as it's very interactive and takes the pressure off of you to do all the marketing on your own. If you have a business model where you are face to face with customers, let them know that you'll happily share their posts once they check-in with a photo. It helps them feel that their opinion matters, and they're often quite happy to help you, in turn. It naturally increases your audience and gets the power of "word of mouth" that social media can naturally provide. Having your customers share about your products and services is much more powerful than you sharing the very same features and benefits.

GIVEAWAYS AND INCENTIVES

Customers are sometimes more likely to engage, share, comment, and interact on social media when they can clearly see what's in it for them. Having a product to give away or some other incentive can help increase your business sales but also increase your activity on social media.

If you're considering this tactic, remember that your audience is busy with their regular lives and will require a good incentive to engage. For example, a $1 savings off your $200 product isn't likely to do much, but $25 could be much more compelling. Think about what would motivate you to take action on an offer as your audience likely needs the same motivation.

SIX TIPS TO A SUCCESSFUL GIVEAWAY OR INCENTIVE ON SOCIAL MEDIA

1. **Identify the ultimate business goal.** Customers generally like giveaways, but as a business, your goals need to be specific so they can be measured. You don't need to share your end goal with your audience, and it's even recommended that you do not. Otherwise, they can become costly expenditures that serve neither you nor the audience.

2. **Follow the terms of service.** It's not worth risking your entire social media presence you are working so hard to build. For example, if the rules say you can't require people to share your post for a giveaway, then don't. Others may do it all the time, but all this shows is they either willing to jeopardize their businesses or just aren't paying attention.

3. **Make it crystal clear what they need to do to enter.** Spell out the specifics of what people need to do to qualify for your giveaway. A lack of clarity only serves to frustrate your audience and create a very different kind of engagement that will have the exact opposite effect of what you're seeking.

4. **Leverage their friends.** Use language in your copy that encourages participants to share details about your giveaway with their friends. For example, adding a line like "Who else needs to know about this?" can get your audience thinking quite specifically about others who could benefit from your offer. The expanded exposure will gain you a larger audience and greater engagement with little to no effort.

5. **Have a deadline.** It almost doesn't even matter how long you run your giveaway, but having a deadline creates genuine scarcity that you can leverage as time runs out.

HERE'S WHY VIDEO BRINGS AMAZING VALUE TO YOUR MESSAGE

Have you ever binged watched videos by the same person on YouTube or on social media? I know I sure have. On one sleepless night a few years ago, I came across Holly Homer of Quirky Momma and was completely transfixed until I felt like I truly knew her. What a joy it was to make a personal, face-to-face connection with her a few months later during a round table discussion at Social Media Marketing World.

Her use of video to expand her brand, Quirky Momma, is a fine demonstration of how you can use this increasingly powerful marketing tool for your own social media efforts. Showing your face on camera allows our audience to get to know us faster than just about any other method. Gone are the days of needing highly produced videos and TV spots costing thousands of dollars in the hopes that a few of the right people will hear your message. Thanks to platforms like YouTube, we've become accustomed to videos crafted on smaller, less expensive cameras and even phones. A quality microphone helps, but even those can be purchased relatively inexpensively.

Add in that most social media platforms now have a live video component for instant broadcasting, and video becomes an even more powerful tool to connect with your audience. The video can stay on the newsfeed for later or repeat viewers, which further enhances the power of your content. Further, the ability to interact with the audience while you're live creates a far more dynamic experience for both you and your viewers that is difficult to duplicate with regular video. It's a surefire way to build trust and rapport with your audience and best of all, it's free.

Facebook Live is currently the most popular for live videos, but other platforms are adopting the strategy—like LinkedIn. The access to these tools means that with just a phone and no fancy devices, you can take advantage of video marketing immediately.

There are undoubtedly readers thinking, *I don't want to go on camera!* It might be a bit nerve-wracking at first, but with practice, it gets much easier, and you'll likely find people are more interested in what you have to say than you might think, particularly if you've spent time identifying the right audience. All you really have to do to master video is smile and make eye contact with the camera. Well, and stay on track with what you want to talk about, but that's where the practice helps, too.

Further, check out these statistics on where video is going:

- Every 30 days there is more online video content that had been uploaded on the Internet than in the past 30 years of TV content
- A Facebook executive predicted that their platform will be all video by 2021
- The average person spends 15 hours each week with digital video
- 92% of mobile users watching video will share it with others
- Cisco predicts that 82% of all Internet traffic in 2022 will be video
- 6 out of 10 people would rather watch online videos than TV
- 94% of respondents in a Facebook survey of 1 million people have a phone in hand while watching TV
- 72% of customers would rather learn about a product from a video as compared to 10% who prefer text
- Social media posts with video have 48% more views
- 80% of consumers believe demonstration videos are helpful when they make purchase decisions
- Social video generates 1,200% more shares than text and image content combined
- 86% of viewers suggest they search YouTube when they need to learn something new

In short, social media and video are here to stay. It's worth it to learn how to leverage the power of both to grow and connect with your audience.

TIPS TO GET THE MOST FROM YOUR LIVE VIDEOS

Live video on social media has become more and more popular over the past several years. Everything from Periscope (now often referred to as Twitter Live), Facebook Live, LinkedIn Live, YouTube Live, and Instagram Live.

Regardless of the platform, here are some ways for you to maximize your live video:

Be consistent on when you go live. We all get used to routine, and our audience is no different. Choosing a specific time and approximate length of your broadcasts trains your audience to expect fresh content, makes it easier for them to plan for it, and they'll be far more likely to watch you live.

Engage with the audience. We all like to be acknowledged, and a simple hello can go a long way to let your audience know you're interested in them. Asking for comments and questions will increase their engagement and give you the chance to respond to them in real-time. This can lead to fantastic discussions, directly helps you know what your audience is thinking, and where they're coming from.

Acknowledge the replay viewers. Not everybody is going to be able to watch your videos live. Simply thanking them for catching the replay and asking for their comments will go a long way to gain their appreciation.

Eyes, sound, and smiles matter. You don't need fancy equipment to do a live broadcast. Even your phone will work if that's all you have. Just make sure you know where the camera is, smile, and speak clearly at a volume people can easily hear and showcase your personality.

Your message matters. From what you say on screen to the copy you create to announce you're going live; you want to communicate your message in a fashion that creates curiosity so people will stop scrolling and watch your video. Tell the audience what's in it for them if they watch.

Call to action. Your audience joined you for instruction, and they need to know what to do next. Even if it's just to tune in next time or to go sign up for something, tell them. Too many business owners miss this step and then wonder why their audiences aren't growing.

Just do it. Nike sure got this one figured out. We all get nervous when we're trying out something new for the first time. We also get better with practice, and you're going to get better, too.

BONUS: THE POWER OF ONE-MINUTE VIDEOS

Check out this gem from Dennis Yu, the founder of Blitzmetrics:

"One-minute videos are micro-touches to build relationships with customers. So why not use Facebook for what it's meant for—to drive the right exposure and engagement? Do vertical videos telling stories, educating customers, and then eventually selling—moving potential customers along via re-marketing sequences."

I had the pleasure of meeting Dennis in person a few years ago when he gave me some additional awesome advice. When I asked him how I could thank him, he said, "Go post a one-minute video on Facebook sharing what you learned and how it helped." I did exactly as he said and also tagged his business page in the post. He then shared my video on his personal Facebook profile, which both exposed me to a new audience and increased recognition to him for the help he had offered me. It may seem small, but it was an easy and powerful win-win for each of us and a great way to communicate on social media.

Here are five simple things that you can do to make your next one-minute video:

1. **Use a little bit of movement to get attention at the start of your videos, even something simple like a wave.** The idea is to cause people to stop scrolling and check out your video.
2. **Smile, make eye contact, and give them a brief explanation of who you are and what you're about to share, preferably in less than ten seconds.** This lets them know what they're going to get out of watching and if it's worth it to them to continue watching.
3. **Deliver the value!**
4. **Ask for engagement, like leaving a comment or a question.**
5. **Have a call to action**. This is different from asking for engagement as we're asking for engagement beyond just the video we've posted so we can continue to build our audience and client list.

This is a great strategy for videos of almost any length. Shorter videos are still recommended so you deliver the value before viewers start dropping off, but you can adjust the length as appropriate for your content and the platform you're using.

Video marketing is well within your reach, and you can start using it even today. One-minute videos are a fantastic way to learn how to do them, and you'll get more comfortable with video as you practice. We suggested in the last section that you compile the ten most common questions you get from your customers. Just the same as if you were to write about them, this is an excellent place to begin. You could create a Top Ten-style of list and create a short video for each point.

Your entertaining and educational videos are a sure-fire way to create rapport with your audience. Breaking it down to smaller pieces will make it that much easier to get started and reduce your stress load. Either way, it's time to take action and show us what you've got.

STAGE FIVE

AUTOMATION AND SMART SYSTEMS

We've sure covered a lot of ground, haven't we? From figuring out our ideal audience and the platforms we should use to the right kind of content and the format in which we share it.

If you're starting to feel a bit overwhelmed, take a deep breath, and know this chapter is going to make your life much easier. We truly don't want social media to take over our lives, and we don't have to. We're about to cover how we can automate much of our process as possible without losing the personal touch. Rest assured we can save many hours along the way so we can still maintain some sanity and enjoy our lives.

You see, I get quite passionate about business owners having systems and automation in place for improved efficiency and scalability. If we only have so many hours in a day, doesn't it just make sense to use them as wisely as we can? Also, who doesn't want to increase what they make in the same amount of time without doing extra work? Isn't that why we started our businesses in the first place?

I digress, but the point is that the more we can systematize and automate our processes, the less work will have to do while getting far better results. Note that there's a difference between systems and automation. We systematize the parts that needed our direct attention and automate the pieces that don't. It's how my executive assistant and I were able to create the smooth-running machine that is my business, Jesus and Sweet Tea podcast. Tools like Trello help us create a beautiful visual of what is happening from finding guests to editing and publishing, saving us precious time, and always keeping us on track.

AUTOMATE THE PROCESS, NOT THE ENGAGEMENT.

The term "automation" can carry a negative connotation. Let's be clear that we are talking about automating how our businesses operation, not relationships. We are wise to use technology to enhance relationships and foolish if we try to replace them.

Reducing Overwhelm

Without systems and automation in place, it's easy to get overwhelmed. We might have our audience figured out but can quickly feel lost if we've not adapted a schedule of when and what to post. Social media then becomes our master as we scramble on what to do, and we stand to lose out on all the benefits we're working so hard to gain.

There are three powerful strategies for systems and automation.

Scheduling Posts

There are many pros to scheduling your posts in advance. It removes the need for you to be online constantly and is particularly useful if you've created a series of related posts. As you study the analytics of your posts, you'll find patterns in which of your content your audience most prefers and when they are likely to consume it. It will involve a bit of trial and error to nail it down, but you will quickly see improvements to your workflow. You'll be able to use your time more effectively and focus more on your creativity.

Facebook has a built-in system for scheduling posts, and there are tools like Agorapulse that allow for scheduling on Instagram, among others. We'll cover a few more of these tools in the next section.

Keep in mind, we can go overboard scheduling too many of our posts. Interaction is still key, so a month's worth of posts on a "set it and forget it" schedule would do nothing to enhance the relationships we're trying to grow. It's still important to show up in real-time with posts and responses. This demonstrates to your audience than you really are there, care about them, and makes a far more favorable impression for your business.

Google Alerts

Our first strategy can still enslave us if we need to monitor responses to our posts constantly. Google Alerts is another fantastic tool to lighten the load.

Setting up notifications for your business name and personal name will alert you anytime you are mentioned on Google or Facebook. This frees you from having to constantly monitor whether people are discussing you and gives you the chance to respond as soon as they do. Obviously, we enjoy when we're spoken of in positive ways, but the ability to handle negativity quickly also helps build our brand and reputation.

Chatbots

Chatbots have gained tremendous popularity on Facebook. Open rates on Facebook Messenger are decidedly higher than email open rates and can automatically deliver information to your audience when they engage with certain posts you've created. Done properly, bots can help build connections and rapport.

Be warned that just like automating too many posts, a "set it and forget it" strategy can do more damage than good. As effective as bots can be, it is wise to either get training on how to use them or hire someone knowledgeable to help you set yours up. It's still important that your audience knows you value relationships and are personable.

Another quick note on automation: connecting all of your social platforms is not a good idea. They might save time, but please review in previous chapters the importance of catering your content to the strengths of each platform you plan to use.

17 TOOLS TO SIMPLIFY YOUR SOCIAL MEDIA MARKETING (AND SAVE YOU HOURS OF YOUR LIFE)

Since the dawn of time, we've been a tool-making species. Even in the digital age, we're making remarkable advancements. I remember back in 2000 using Adobe Photoshop on a Macintosh computer to remove the background behind a tennis racket one pixel at a time. Now, we just click one button, and it's done. Oh, the time I could have saved way back when.

There are so many great tools to simplify our lives and businesses that it can now almost be overwhelming in the opposite direction. What follows is a list of tools and resources I personally used to grow my businesses with social media marketing. They range from graphic creation and time management to research and communications.

I have included a few of my affiliate links for some of these, which doesn't affect anything on your end, but I do need to share that in the name of full disclosure. If you see an affiliate link, it means that I have been using it and am very pleased with the product.

Canva

Used by non-designers and professionals alike, this is a fantastic website-based graphic design tool that's also available on iOS and Android. They provide a simple drag-and-drop format and access to many photographs, graphics, templates, and fonts.

The free version is exceptionally powerful, and should you find yourself using it consistently, the paid version is well worth the investment for the additional time-saving tools. For example, you can create a graphic for Instagram, and with one click, it will reformat the graphic for a Facebook post with little to no additional tweaks. As a long-time graphic designer, it's a game-changer that can greatly enhance your productivity.

Google Calendar

If you want to be successful with social media and your business in general, you need to be well organized and manage your time appropriately. This free, cloud-based time management and scheduling calendar simplifies this essential task, is available on IOS and Android, and updates your calendar across all your devices at one time. I find it particularly useful when I am on the go to track my responsibilities and appointments as well as schedule my future social media tasks.

Agorapulse

Agorapulse is a social community and moderation tool that centralizes all your social networks in a unified interface so you can manage all of it from one location. It helps you track how many comments, messages, and tweets you have received so you can readily read, reply, delegate, or tag as appropriate. It saves a tremendous amount of time logging in and out of all your platforms, so you can easily monitor conversations and engage in real-time with your audience while you free up time for other tasks like speaking with potential clients or helping existing clients. Get a FREE 2-week trial here: www.sweetteasocialmarketing.com/agorapulse.

I personally use it to monitor Facebook, Twitter, Instagram, LinkedIn, and YouTube. Publishing content is very user-friendly, and their printable reports are exceptionally detailed and easy to download.

Type O Rama

This is a beautiful app for iPhone and iPad that lets you transform your text into graphic designs with a few different customizations. The workflow is simple, and I often find Type O Rama to be the app that I use when I am on the go making graphics.

Adobe Spark

This design suite from Adobe consists of three apps called Spark Page, Spark Post, and Spark Video. With this toolset, you can create simple and quick videos from scratch in seconds easily on your phone or your PC, including the use of their free music. The free version is somewhat limited in fonts, backgrounds, and themes, yet still excels for storytelling and branding. The paid version opens up many additional options, but you can still get far with the free version.

Google Drive

Google Drive is a great resource for file storage and data synchronization. It's particularly helpful for sharing files with clients or other team members. The mobile app allows you the same control over your data as you have on a PC, meaning you have full access even when you're on the go.

Voxer

Voxer is a free walkie-talkie app for smartphones. The live push-to-talk and voice-messaging system makes for simple, rapid communications, particularly among team members. Beyond them, I personally only use it with a handful of dear friends, mentors, and VIP clients. Offering Voxer access can be a great upsell if you're looking to find consulting clients.

Marco Polo

Marco Polo is a video messaging and video hosting service mobile app. Think Voxer, but with video. I personally use this less than Voxer but still find it handy at times. You might like this better if you prefer to see who you're communicating with.

Zoom

Zoom is an easy-to-use, robust, and stable communications platform for video and audio conferencing with a simple learning curve and phenomenal customer service. The basic plan includes unlimited one-on-one meetings, forty-minute group meetings, and screen sharing so you can share what's on your screen for trainings and the like. You can also record the conversations for review or to share with others, which is super handy when you're consulting. There are add-on options for hosting webinars, additional recording time, reporting, and a scheduler to enhance your operations. In fact, this is how I record most of my podcast interviews. You can go to my link here: www.sweetteasocialmarketing.com/zoom.

Hashtagify.me

This is a free hashtag service/discovery engine. It provides basic analytical data that allows you to research which hashtags are best suited to your goals. This is particularly important when you're developing your social media marketing plan on platforms like Instagram and Twitter. Facebook uses them as well, but only in moderation, making it wise to study the hashtag culture on different platforms.

Social Insider

This is an analytical tool that helps you optimize your social media strategy, spot trends in advance, and measure your performance against your competition.

Buzz Sumo

Buzz Sumo is a powerful online tool for researching what content is popular by topic or on any website. They do have paid services, but your first few searches each day are totally free, which is often enough to help you find the inspiration for content to use for social media posts to leverage popular topics.

MailChimp

This is an excellent email marketing automation tool that you can also use to create landing pages. They are free up through your first 2,000 subscribers and can scale with you as you grow.

ConvertKit

As your email list grows, you'll want to consider other options for automation. For all the email platforms I've tried, ConvertKit is my favorite for their automation and broadcast capabilities and reasonable pricing. You can access my link at www.sweettea-socialmarketing.com/convertkit.

Dropbox

This is a file hosting service similar to Google Drive. I like both but find this easier to use on mobile devices and for larger files. With shared folders, I can easily record podcasts on the go, instantly upload the file, and my team can access it immediately for editing and distribution. It's a great resource for easy access to your content.

ClickFunnels

ClickFunnels is an online platform for building sales funnels, helping businesses market, sell, and deliver products online. This isn't my area of expertise, but it's a popular platform with a strong community, and I've found excellent people to assist me short-term to get my funnels running correctly. It takes some time to learn, but they do offer a 14-day free trial to get your feet wet before you make a purchase decision. It's very effective for capturing data that helps optimize funnel performance. You can check out my link here: www.sweetteasocialmarketing.com/clickfunnels.

Acuity

This scheduling tool is super easy to use and can save countless hours of planning time by allowing people to schedule their own appointments with you. You can create many varieties of appointment types and can also require people to pay you upfront before they can secure their times. It syncs well with Google Calendar and automatically monitors when you're available so it won't interfere with the rest of your schedule, allowing you to continue both your business and personal life uninterrupted. You can check out my link at www.sweetteasocialmarketing.com/acuity.

Each of these tools can help you systematize and automate your business. Improving your processes helps in better communications with your team and achieving goals, all while easily scaling your operations, minimizing overwhelm, and delivering a stronger impact. Who knows, you might even have fun along the way.

HOW BATCHING MAKES OUR SOCIAL MEDIA SO MUCH EASIER

If you're like me, interruptions drive you absolutely crazy and make it very difficult to remain focused on the task at hand. Rest assured, I love my family, but when my kids and husband are asking me questions fifteen times in less than thirty minutes while I'm trying to work, it makes me a little crazy.

The point remains that staying focused is crucial to our success in business. Too often, we can sit down at the computer with seventeen browsers open, Facebook and email on even more tabs, the phone ringing, text messages beeping at us, all while we need to be concentrating on the content we're actually trying to create. Can you see how this leads to even more distractions? It's highly ineffective and wastes huge amounts of time.

A far better method is to turn off the phone for a while, close all those extra tabs you don't need, create a list of the tasks that need to accomplish, and batch out the time to get them accomplished.

Your list might vary, but here are tasks for which I specifically plan my time:

Content Planning

I set out the list of topics I want to cover over the coming weeks or months, create a rough plan for when I want to share them, and figure out what kind of posts I want to create. This is when we consider things like the top ten questions our customers ask and build from there. We might change the order of what we plan, but it still lays a foundation for what needs to be researched, created, and published.

Content Creation

Planning and creating are often separate processes, particularly when we're thinking longer-term. The creation phase is when we curate the material we want to use, including links, video, graphics, and anything else that supports our content.

Video Creation

I do love making videos. I'll schedule the time I need to get ready including hair and makeup so I both feel and look good on camera. (Guys might not have to worry about makeup, but maybe go run a comb through your hair and get in a quick shave.) If I shoot more than one video at a time, I often change shirts and pick a different place in my house or office for variety. Wherever I end up, I still like to get as many videos done at a time so they're just done and off my plate.

These are just a few examples of batching and how you can use your time so much more effectively. This will make you far more efficient when you have a team and even more so when you're running solo. Either way, remember that time is the one resource we can't renew, so we are wise to use it effectively.

A SIMPLE AND SMART SOCIAL MEDIA STRATEGY PLAN

In my Social Thrive Business Academy, we break down your entire social media plan into twenty concise steps. In fact, we've skimmed most of them throughout the book and go deep into the nuts and bolts inside the Academy. We like to think of the community there as family, and continually help one another so all can be successful. Our strategies are time tested and work whether your business is service or product-based, online or offline, brand new or seasoned, or any combination thereof. All of it boils down to the same twenty steps that we follow.

1. Define your business goals

Social media can help you achieve your goals, but they first need to be defined. Why are you really doing this? Take your time on this and be honest.

2. Know your audience

We've covered this extensively throughout this book, and it's well worth repeating. Who are they? What are their habits? What are their needs? What are their problems? The better you understand them, the easier it is to provide the solution to their problem. If you've not reached out to your audience before, you can create a survey for free with Google forms with a few simple questions to find out. The data will give you a place to start from, and you can build upon that as you go.

3. Know your expertise

The adage of "fake it 'til you make it" isn't going to cut it in social media. Yes, we all have to start somewhere, but you won't be able to pretend to be something you're not for long. Honesty is crucial in this arena, so you're far better off assessing your skills and experience and growing from there. Bring these to the table with you so you can best serve your audience and you'll find all that you do is much more fulfilling.

4. Know what sets you apart

In short, what makes you different from your competition? Why is someone going to come to you instead of someone else? We don't need to be wildly different from everyone else, but if we're the same as everyone else, then we're going to have a difficult time finding and leading an audience.

Further, know that trying to be everything for everyone is a sure-fire recipe for disaster. Focus on your expertise, share what makes you unique, and continue from there. It will be far easier in the long run, and you'll have a more enjoyable experience.

5. Nail down your offers

If we don't have anything to offer, we don't make a sale, and if we don't make a sale, we don't make money. It seems pretty simple, yet we've all seen examples on social media where it's near impossible to figure out what is actually being sold. Make sure you have this well-defined to avoid confusion for both you and your customers and to get them contacting you to do business.

6. Create social media goals that help you accomplish your business goals

Everything you do in social media should help you get closer to accomplishing your business goals. Set realistic goals that are will stretch you, measure your results, and adjust accordingly. The journey is more important than the end goal, but without them, we'll be without direction.

7. Pick the social media platform of choice

Armed with the knowledge of your audience and your area of expertise, go back to Stage 3 and review which platform makes the most sense for finding your audience. Remember that what works on one platform may not fit the culture of another, so it is wise to master one platform before moving on to more, and even then, we must be careful on how we divide our time.

8. Identify your content

It might seem easier to share everybody else's content, but that doesn't do much to create your own voice. If you're still wondering where to start, you can always go back to the top ten questions you get asked by your customers and create a post for each of those.

9. Sort your content into buckets

Think of this like batching your content so you can stay better organized. Buckets can include themes like inspiration, questions for your audience, questions from your audience, behind the scenes, offerings, customer spotlights, testimonials, and anything else you can think of that's relevant to your audience and needs.

10. Use the 85/15 rule

This is a custom spinoff of the 80/20 rule in which I suggest you spend 85% of your time adding value, helping your audience, letting them get to know who you are, and showcasing customers and other businesses, and the other 15% making your offers like inviting people to buy your goods and services. This will be a far more successful way to build relationships and connections as opposed to so many Facebook business pages that spam their audiences for sales 100% of the time.

11. Engage and respond on social media

Social media, by definition, suggests interaction with your audience. Make sure to answer questions for your audience, encourage conversation, and partake in their comments as well. Acknowledging and engaging your audience will go far in developing those relationships.

12. Put out your offers

I strongly believe that social media is first about building relationships and earning the trust of your audience, but we still have a business to run. We can certainly ask for sales sometimes, but offers can include invitations to an email list, phone calls, giveaways, or other things that help drive engagement. Assuming you've built trust appropriately, your audience won't mind you asking for something in return.

13. Follow up with excellence

Have you ever heard the phrase "the fortune is in the follow-up"? It's true. Even more important is how you conduct the follow-up.

Like all things in business, make sure your follow-up is also conducted with excellence. This is when you're most like to create actual clients from potential ones and deserves your greatest attention. If someone sends you a tweet asking to learn more about your business, respond to them with the needed information. But even consider making them a thirty-second video thanking them for reaching out. Ask them the appropriate level of questions, demonstrate that you care about them, and show them how you will be serving them, and you're far more likely to get the sale. Otherwise, you're leaving money on the table.

14. Spotlight happy customers and make them the hero

This is pure social gold. Letting your customers be your heroes showcases the value you provide, and your customers will enjoy being the center of attention. This is an excellent strategy emphasized by author and influencer Donald Miller of *Building a Storybrand*. They become ambassadors to your audience and offer social proof of what you can do for them. Having others talk about you saves you from having to talk about yourself.

15. Be visible

Use social media to get in front of people so they get to know you. This doesn't mean we overtly get in people's faces, but it's okay to share about what we're up to. It makes you more relatable, which then helps you stay top of mind and can even lead to referrals, new leads, and people asking to work with you or do business with you.

16. Take offline events and conversations onto social media

Undoubtedly, you will be in situations where the people you're around aren't online. For example, I was at a chamber of commerce breakfast and recorded a quick fifteen-second pan of the room filled with all the business owners and leaders from the area. I later shared the video on my Facebook business page with a comment about how much I enjoyed connecting with all the local leadership. Additionally, if you meet someone at a conference that you really enjoy, connect with them right there on LinkedIn or on your social media platform of choice.

Actions like this help show you're invested in building up community and other businesses. It helps bring visibility to a larger network and benefits so many more people. There are countless opportunities to highlight activities that aren't necessarily online.

17. Take social media offline

This is similar to the last point in which we link social media to offline events, only this time we use it in reverse. For example, you can use your platform to invite your audience to local events or discovery calls. These are great ways to increase engagement for activities better served elsewhere other than social media. The next time someone sends a message asking a question, write them back with an answer to their question, but also give them your direct number to call to answer anything else they may need. It makes for a nice personal touch.

18. Serve your customers like crazy

This might seem obvious, but the way some businesses treat people would suggest otherwise. It's important to remember that at the end of the day, all business is about people, and our services and products are just the medium through which we exchange value. This is true whether we're just getting started or have massive teams working for us. Think of your own experiences with customer services, what you did and didn't like, and realize your customers will think the same of you. It's crucial to do the right thing at all times, particularly if you want to continue to grow your business.

19. Be generous

This goes hand-in-hand with the last point. Being generous with your customers can often be as simple as treating them with kindness, grace, and patience. It's a cliché to suggest we under-promise and over-deliver, but it's still a good philosophy to incorporate into our businesses because it does much to increase the loyalty from our audience.

20. Spotlight other businesses

There are many good businesses out there. Network with them, highlight them, and share their strengths, and in return, they may offer you the same. A phrase I love is "rising tides lift all boats," and we can do much more for people when we all work together.

And that's the magic sauce behind all that we cover in my Social Thrive Business Academy. In short, treating others how you'd like to be treated shouldn't have to be limited to just our personal interactions. Applying the same ideas to how we conduct ourselves professionally will build enduring businesses with loyal fan bases, and social media is a fantastic tool to achieve these ends.

STAGE SIX

LEGACY AND KINGDOM IMPACT

My husband and I are Christians and have been long-time admirers of Billy Graham. We grew up listening to him, and I remember reading a book by him about angels when I was in high school. We were amazed at his ability to fill stadiums as he preached his message about the gospel. To this day, we enjoy stories about his family and the positive impact he had around the world.

A few years ago, we decided to take our kids to The Billy Graham Library in Charlotte, North Carolina. He was such a wise man, and it still fills my heart with joy thinking of his ability to influence even years after he has since gone to heaven to be with Jesus.

Regardless of whether you are a Christian or not, there is no argument that Billy Graham built a legacy that has far outlasted the work he did while he was here on earth. His example is powerful, which leads to an important question I want to ask you:

How do you want to be remembered?

Are you just looking to make a few extra bucks with your business? If so, then this section might not be important to you. We've covered plenty enough in the book for you to use social media to grow your business and odds are good you will do quite well.

However, if you want to leave a bigger mark on this world, please keep reading. Rest assured that you can use your business to create a legacy that will get passed down through generations so each may benefit from the fruits of your labor. It requires bigger and long-term thinking and leaving behind limiting beliefs, particularly those of ourselves. There is a Chinese proverb that suggests the best time to plant a tree is twenty years ago and that the next best time is right now. It's no different for your business, and unless you have a time machine that you're not telling anyone about, there will never be a better time to get started.

It sure sounds good, but you might be asking, "How do I leave a legacy?"

Fortunately, it isn't all that complicated. Central to all of it is understanding that your entire audience, everyone you ever meet or interact with, wherever they come from and what they want out of life are much the same as you and me. They have their own struggles, fears, joys, and passions and show up to do the best they can with what they've got every day. They might approach things differently than us, but that's what makes this world the amazing and diverse place that it is.

Here's a snapshot of how I choose to conduct myself, whether it's personally, professionally, through my church activities, or with my family—everywhere and with everyone. I've said it more than once throughout the book that all business is ultimately about people, and putting them first is how we can create a lasting legacy and affect change far and wide.

1. Be kind, it's courageous
2. Pay it forward
3. Give to give

4. Offer help expecting nothing in return
5. Live the golden rule
6. Integrity always wins
7. Anticipate greatness
8. Talk about greatness on social media
9. Stand for something
10. Include what you stand for in your messaging
11. Be vulnerable
12. Be transparent
13. Say yes when you can and no when you can't
14. Encourage your customers, team, and family
15. Mentor someone for free
16. Acknowledge what others overlook
17. Smile daily
18. Apologize as needed and mean it
19. Say please and thank you
20. Invite God to help you start every single day
21. Show gratitude when people least expect it and over-deliver
22. Genuinely care for others
23. Be an advocate for causes you are passionate about
24. Think big picture and take action to make it happen
25. Be human in how you market

Truett Cathy, the founder of Chick-fil-A, embodies these principles exceedingly well. The purpose statement for the company reads, "To glorify God by being a faithful steward of all that is entrusted to us and to have a positive influence on all who come in contact with Chick-fil-A." In spite of pressure and pushbacks, he made the decision that Chick-fil-A will be closed on Sundays. Recognizing the money he could likely have made for the company by staying open, he chooses people before profits and family over business, and it reflects in the entire company culture.

The next time you choose to partake in that amazing chicken, fantastic sweet tea, and perfectly salted waffle fries (yes, I'm a Chick-fil-A raving fan), note how they say, "It's my pleasure" and offer a genuine smile as they serve you. You don't have to be a Christian to note that their culture aims to serve a higher purpose and wants to help people.

To whatever you choose to attribute their success, it's worth noting that according to *Entrepreneur, Inc.* Chick-fil-A makes more per restaurant than McDonald's, Starbucks, and Subway combined—and they are closed on Sundays.

That is legacy. That is what it is to leave an impact on the world. They're growing like wildfire, and you can, too.

GOLDEN RULE:
Stand for Something

As business owners, we are in a leadership position and have the opportunity to stand up for causes we believe in and serving others. Honestly, it's fun.

One of my mentors, Stu McLaren, says it so well, "Stand for something. It won't resonate with everyone, and that's okay. But be okay showing up in your business and standing for something."

The ability to help others is one we are wise to exercise, and let's be real, there's a marketing perspective to it as well. One human showing up to help another is a beautiful thing, particularly in a world that appears to be drowning in so much negativity. It's okay to use your social media efforts to highlight these good things happening, and I even encourage it. It gives your audience a glimpse of the real you and forges stronger relationships because you're showing up authentically.

In my own business, I've had the privilege of helping causes like the work happening at Clarity Solutions for Women, a crisis pregnancy center in Elizabethtown, Kentucky. Even though my business wasn't an official sponsor, my family and I helped with a 5K walk they were hosting as a fundraiser, and we took lots of pictures we posted on social media. It helped draw attention to their organization, and we had a wonderful time.

I've also been able to show support through my businesses for great organizations like Feeding America, Kentucky's Heartland in Elizabethtown, Kentucky, Alzheimer's Association of Greater Kentucky and Southern Indiana, Fighting Human Trafficking, Fostering and Adopting.

Think about organizations you could work with that could benefit from your help. The opportunities are out there if you take the time to look. You can make a bigger impact this way, and the benefits would be mutual. A rising tide raises all ships, remember, and we can help raise the tide.

A SPECIAL NOTE TO CHRISTIAN BUSINESS OWNERS

Customers, clients, and the very people you deal with every single day are varied. Some know Jesus, and some don't. If you have the love of Jesus in your heart, I encourage you to share that light through your business in the way you operate with integrity, grace, mercy, love, and kindness for others. Not everyone will understand, but they can certainly feel it when you share your heart this way. You may be the only light some will get to see or know.

You don't need to have massive success or be perfectly beautiful, skilled, or flawless. None of us are, really, and God only asks us to be willing. What gives me comfort is knowing that we can release the pressure of trying to do it all by ourselves and just lean into God and ask him to do his work in us.

Be encouraged.
Ephesians 2:8–9

A FINAL WORD

If this book has touched you, I'd love to hear from you. Please share success stories, challenges, and inspirations by emailing them to me at heather@sweetteasocialmarketing.com or by getting social with me and using the hashtag #thegoldenrules.

Until we meet again, I pray that your business or non-profit would be blessed beyond measure and that you continue to take action and show up ready to serve your audience well. If you just read this book but don't take action, you will not benefit from the great results that await you.

I see you.

You've got this.

WHY LEGACY AND IMPACTING OTHERS MATTERS

Assuming you've read the entire book, let's agree that we're both business builders looking to leverage social media to amplify our voice and grow our audiences, so we want to increase our profits. When we put people ahead of profits, choosing to serve and care for them, everything else manages to fall into place. Of course, you need to ask for sales and generate an income, but if we care about money more than people, neither will show up in great quantities or stay for long. We will leave an impression on others regardless of what we do. Can you honestly think of a reason to not make it a good one?

It doesn't matter if you're starting out or have 5,000 employees. It's even okay if your primary goal is to create just a bit more income to help pay the bills or take that trip to Disney World. We still have the power to affect change in people's lives, to help them improve their circumstances or outlook, and it's my sincere desire that you create an impact like that.

This definitely gets personal for me. Whether it's through offline or social media, I love the opportunity I have to work with my clients, the audiences I get to speak with at events, and the causes I like to support. As my businesses grow, so does my flexibility for my family and for the people I can increasingly serve. We are all given the same 24 hours in a day, but the more we grow our income, the easier it is to share. Infusing this mindset from the beginning helps form the entire culture of our own businesses, and social media makes it so much easier to spread our message.

Your message will resonate with your core audience, and it will naturally grow from there. In my own case, I've been able to help advance causes for foster families, adoption, and against human trafficking. I include a side note in my proposals to potential clients that a percentage of the proceeds in my company go toward these causes to both increase awareness and let them know their money will help serve others.

There's nothing that says you must do these things, but I can personally attest to the community growth it fosters. During a mission trip that my daughter and I went on in 2018, we each decided to sponsor a child we met there, and I chose to involve Social Thrive Business Academy in the sponsorship. Everyone was delighted to know that a portion of their monthly investment was having an impact on a sweet little girl across the globe in Guatemala. It brought us closer together as a community, and we're constantly looking for other ways we can serve. It's a lot of fun and feels amazing to help others.

This is legacy building. It's taking the resources we've been blessed with and looking out for others where and when we can. A rising tides lift all ships.

It can even be a competitive advantage. That might sound crass, but as the world draws closer, many people are becoming more socially conscious. When they are presented with a service or product from two different companies that are similar in price, quality, and experience, the cause a company serves to advance can often sway a purchasing decision. It's much easier to stand with a business that wants to do good in the world.

It can open the door to conversations you might not otherwise enjoy. In my own case, I recently had a gentleman reach out to me that had been following me for eighteen months on

LinkedIn. We had the commonality of being on school boards, and he was looking for someone who could do some training about team building. It wasn't my knowledge of social media, my leadership experience, or my master's degree that made the difference. Those were all important factors, but he reached out to me because of the content I share about combining faith and business. It's who I am and what I like to talk about, and we are a good fit because I was being myself on social media.

I share this because I don't want you to underestimate the interests that you have, any of your volunteer experience, or the causes that tug at your heart. They can all lead to new conversations and relationships and be factors that bring you new business and referrals.

CONCLUSION

Phew!

We've covered a lot of information in this book that you can directly apply to your business and your social media marketing efforts. When I first started using social media for business growth in 2011, it was all trial and error and seeing what worked and what didn't. I have only been using social media for business since then, but it's an extension of what I have been doing in digital marketing, sales, and relationship marketing since 2000. It's simply a tool to expand our reach, and we need not complicate it any more than that.

What you've just read is a battle-tested strategy with practical applications that I've been able to leverage through my own businesses and those of hundreds of my clients. These strategies also work for non-profits and local businesses, whether they are service or product-based or whether they are online or offline.

To get the most out of what you've read, this is where I recommend you start:

1. Get crystal clear on the strong foundation of your business model so that you know what your business is, what your customers want, where to find them, and how you can serve them.
2. Identify your unique story, set yourself apart from your competition, show up on the social media platform that best matches your audience, and tell your story through with great copy, photos, and video.
3. Show up on social media with genuine value, with your own personality and style.
4. Cultivate, nurture, foster, and grow authentic relationships with your ideal dream customer and those around you that you want to know (peers, media, etc.).
5. Implement automation and systems in your business so you aren't a slave to social media. Time is your most precious asset, so get organized and leverage tools that allow you to be more productive.
6. Leave a legacy in all things. Incorporate the legacy into your messaging on social media so you can resonate with more people and expand your ability to serve through your own unique gifts and talents.

And please always remember:

YOU'VE GOT THIS! I BELIEVE IN YOU!

STILL LOOKING FOR HELP?

I'd be honored to help you! Here are the ways I can best serve:

INTERNATIONAL KEYNOTE SPEAKER ABOUT SOCIAL MEDIA FOR BUSINESS GROWTH

I've spent the last twenty years in the digital marketing space and have enjoyed sharing my stories and experiences on dozens of stages from Mexico, India, South Carolina, Ohio, Missouri, California, Utah, Arizona, Florida, to North Carolina. I am able to communicate with professionals, business owners and leaders on how my signature S.O.C.I.A.L. framework can help you soar with social media marketing to create a positive impact for business growth.

To book me to speak, visit sweetteasocialmarketing.com/speaker

SOCIAL THRIVE BUSINESS ACADEMY

This is my monthly membership for Christian business owners who are looking for complete training on how to leverage social media to grow a business or non-profit. My top two goals in this membership are to help make Jesus famous and to help you grow using social media marketing in your business. If you are the sole person responsible for social media in your business, you will love the accountability + community + training. Or if you need the person in your company to get hands-on training and have consistent access/resources about social media marketing, this is a great opportunity. I know your time is precious, so we intentionally keep the training concise and clear and show you step-by-step what to do to incorporate smart social media strategies that work to grow your business.

Visit joinsocialthrive.com to join!

LET'S CONNECT ON SOCIAL MEDIA AND ONLINE

Here's where you can find me, Heather Heuman, on social media and my website.

- sweetteasocialmarketing.com
- facebook.com/SweetTeaSocialMarketing
- facebook.com/blessedbusinessmom
- linkedin.com/in/heatherheuman
- instagram.com/heatherheuman
- twitter.com/heatherheuman
- pinterest.com/heatherheuman
- sweetteasocialmarketing.com/youtube

ADDITIONAL FREE RESOURCES

31-DAY SOCIAL MEDIA CONTENT CALENDAR:
sweetteasocialmarketing.com/contentcalendar

HOW TO GROW YOUR PRODUCT OR SERVICE-BASED BUSINESS WITH FACEBOOK:
sweetteasocialmarketing.com/growyourbiz

JOIN MY GROUP: SOCIAL MEDIA FOR CHRISTIAN BUSINESS OWNERS:
sweetteasocialmarketing.com/freegroup

CHECKLIST: GROWING YOUR BUSINESS WITH FACEBOOK SO YOU CAN MAKE A BIGGER KINGDOM IMPACT:
sweetteasocialmarketing.com/freechecklist

LISTEN TO MY PODCAST: Business, Jesus and Sweet Tea (Also available on iTunes.)
sweetteasocialmarketing.com/podcast

GET VISIBLE! USE THE OFFICIAL CUSTOM HASHTAG FOR THE BOOK - #thegoldenrules

Post a one-minute video on social media about how this book is helping you in your business and use the hashtag #thegoldenrules

- If you post it on Twitter or Instagram, mention @heatherheuman so that I can get notified. I'll gladly ENGAGE with your post.
- If you post it on LinkedIn, be sure to send me a connection request and let me know!
- If you post it on Facebook, be sure to mention @ SweetTeaSocialMarketing in the post so that I get notified. I'll gladly SHARE your post and be social with you!

WHAT I WANT EVERYONE THAT READS THIS BOOK TO DO:

Post a photo of yourself holding the book on social media and tell me how the book is helping you. Use the hashtag #thegoldenrules

CPSIA information can be obtained
at www.ICGtesting.com
Printed in the USA
LVHW031949261119
638523LV00002B/268/P